I0029288

Hidden Dangers

Subtle Signs of Failing Schools

Betsy Gunzelmann

Rowman & Littlefield Education
Lanham, Maryland • Toronto • Plymouth, UK
2008

Published in the United States of America
by Rowman & Littlefield Education
A Division of Rowman & Littlefield Publishers, Inc.
A wholly owned subsidary of The Rowman & Littlefield Publishing
Group, Inc.
4501 Forbes Boulevard, Suite 200, Lanham, Maryland 20706
www.rowmaneducation.com

Estover Road
Plymouth PL6 7PY
United Kingdom

Copyright © 2008 by Betsy Gunzelmann

All rights reserved. No part of this publication may be reproduced,
stored in a retrieval system, or transmitted in any form or by any
means, electronic, mechanical, photocopying, recording, or otherwise,
without the prior permission of the publisher.

British Library Cataloguing in Publication Information Available

Library of Congress Cataloging-in-Publication Data

Gunzelmann, Betsy, 1952–
  Hidden dangers : subtle signs of failing schools / Betsy Gunzelmann.
      p. cm.
  Includes bibliographical references.
  ISBN-13: 978-1-57886-689-2 (hardcover : alk. paper)
  ISBN-13: 978-1-57886-690-8 (pbk. : alk. paper)
  ISBN-10: 1-57886-689-8 (hardcover : alk. paper)
  ISBN-10: 1-57886-690-1 (pbk. : alk. paper)
  1. School management and organization–United States. 2.
Education–United States–Evaluation. I. Title.

  LB2805.G855 2008
  371.2 — dc22

                                                    2007026061

⊗™ The paper used in this publication meets the minimum requirements
of American National Standard for Information Sciences — Permanence of
Paper for Printed Library Materials, ANSI/NISO Z39.48-1992.
Manufactured in the United States of America.

To my mother, Mary Gunzelmann, a loving parent and guiding teacher, and to my son, Matt, who is a constant joy and inspiration.

Life is a journey: our task is to make sense out of our experiences so that others might benefit from what we have learned.

Contents

Foreword

The timing of *Hidden Dangers: Subtle Signs of Failing Schools* is phenomenal, bringing with it both good and bad information for us to reflect on. The bad news is, sadly, that our American schools are failing to meet the educational needs of our nation's diverse set of learners. The good news is that *Hidden Dangers* arrives in time for the 2008 U.S. presidential election. Candidates will strive to have an influential voice on a very needed nationwide education reform. Those who read this book will be privy to knowing major, but largely hidden, issues that are perpetuating our declining school system; in addition, they will benefit from learning the surefire ways that Dr. Betsy Gunzelmann recommends we use to rebuild our schools.

Gunzelmann explains in the preface that she wrote *Hidden Dangers: Subtle Signs of Failing Schools* to make us aware of the problems within our educational system that tend to go overlooked. Gunzelmann asks a question that has been on many of our minds for years, namely, what happens to children's wonderful qualities of curiosity, playfulness, creativity, and an eagerness to learn? These traits are suppressed and, after a few years in school, all but disappear. Hidden dangers are inherent in many of the day-to-day school issues that we currently take for granted. Readers will have their eyes opened to hazards that they did not even know existed or just assumed were actually helpful approaches.

It is likely that Dr. Gunzelmann will come to be regarded as the education reformer of the early 21st century. Gunzelmann sees the American school system like it really is and boldly states the issues.

Gunzelmann sees through the popular political jargon of our time, and she is indeed brave enough to confront the large physical, social, and emotional hidden dangers that loom large in our schools. *Hidden Dangers* would be an important book if it only pointed out the areas where our schools are taking wrong turns; however, it also provides attainable solutions—Dr. Gunzelmann recommends and explains specific changes that we can all start to incorporate in working toward a healthy school climate.

Gunzelmann's book is a call to action. It reminds me of a quote from Bob Dylan's 1965 song "It's Alright (I'm Only Bleeding)": "He not busy being born is busy dying." Now, it is our American schools that are bleeding. Those of us who care need to begin by helping politicians, school administrators, teachers, parents, the students, the media, and the American public see the hidden dangers that lurk in our schools.

I am eager to share Dr. Gunzelmann's book with my students at Rivier College because they are the future regular and special education teachers of tomorrow. Gunzelmann shines a spotlight on large problems facing our schools today that are contributing to our current educational crisis. My students and I will ponder why the boys in the American school systems are falling behind the girls, and we will examine the ways that *Hidden Dangers* recommends using the latest neurobiological research to help our boys live up to their greatest potential. We will look deeply at why and how students are labeled, and we will critically weigh the benefits versus the stress caused on our American school system by the myriad of tests that we currently give our students. We will examine ways to make our classrooms feel safe and supportive to each individual student.

I am eager for the politicians to get hold of *Hidden Dangers* and to commit to use this work to lay the foundation for correcting our educational problems. I am optimistic that we as a society of concerned parents, teachers, administrators, and politicians will see the dangers facing our schools today. I am optimistic that we will use the strategies recommended in *Hidden Dangers* to make the necessary changes in our schools. Thank you, Dr. Gunzelmann, for writing this book. We all need to heed your call for action by working toward developing an American school system where all students are respected as individuals, where they are expected to do their best work, and where they are allowed to thrive in a productive and safe school environment.

Diane Connell
Professor, Special Education
Director, Graduate Programs in Learning Disabilities
Rivier College
Nashua, New Hampshire

Preface

Hidden Dangers: Subtle Signs of Failing Schools is the culmination of years of solid teaching, testing, and counseling experience. This knowledge, combined with a well-researched perspective, brings me to an understanding of our educational system from the viewpoint of those who are poorly served by our schools. Many of our students are falling through the cracks, at risk of failing, dropping out, or tuning out. The stories of these children lead us to a new understanding for the problems that we are seeing in our schools, and if we listen carefully, we may even find some solutions.

During President Reagan's leadership in 1983, the *A Nation at Risk* report was published. This report identified the urgent situation in our public schools at that time. According to Tirozzi and Uro (1997),

> by the mid-1980s, a series of studies demonstrated that the performance of U.S. students lagged significantly behind that of students in other countries. By this new standard, the need for education reform was as urgent, if not more so, at the end of the 1980s as it was at the beginning of the decade. (p. 241)

Our schools continue to experience problems despite numerous political attempts to remedy the situation. Each administration since Reagan has been aware of educational problems and has attempted to implement its own fixes. Former president George H. W. Bush led the Charlottesville Education Summit. President Bill Clinton developed the Goal's 2000 Educate America Act. President George W. Bush developed the No Child Left Behind Act in an attempt to solve the educational crisis in our schools. All have made sincere attempts, but all have fallen short of their goals and even created new problems for our schools.

Educational reform in the United States to date has focused on higher standards, increased accountability, standardized testing practices, equal opportunities, and improved curriculum. All these so-called improvements sound convincing, yet we are still seeing many of our children failing, as well as higher dropout rates and discontent.

We've known for some time that our schools have been in trouble and that many of our children were not keeping up educationally with children from many other countries around the world. According to E. D. Hirsch (2006),

> we score low among developed nations in international comparisons of science, math, and reading. This news is in fact more alarming than most people realize, since our students perform relatively worse on international comparisons the longer they stay in our schools. (p. 1; see also Hirsch, 1996)

Microsoft's Bill Gates (2005) agrees with Hirsch's analysis on this issue:

> When I compare our high schools to what I see when I'm traveling abroad, I am terrified for our workforce of tomorrow. In math and science, our 4th graders are among the top students in the world. By 8th grade, they're in the middle of the pack. By 12th grade, U.S. students are scoring near the bottom of all industrialized nations. (p. 3)

Gates goes on to say, "We have one of the highest high school dropout rates in the industrialized world" (p. 3). Furthermore, we continue to see a discrepancy between children from different socioeconomic levels, which Jonathan Kozol (1991) portrays so poignantly in his book *Savage Inequities*.

I felt compelled to write this book to alert school administrators, teachers, psychologists, parents, children, and the concerned general public to take a closer look at the problems within our schools from a different perspective, one that identifies hidden issues that contribute to the downward spiral. There are numerous hidden dangers within our schools that are needlessly compounding the crisis that we are witnessing. We now do not see just mediocre performance but an attitude of indifference and an expectation of youth to passively learn, and our schools and public policies have inadvertently contributed to the educational problems of our youth.

Certainly, there are many youth who do not care about their education, and the schools cannot be blamed for all problems in our society. Yet, I do believe that most children begin their school years full of creativity and an interest in learning. They want to learn to read, write, and discover knowledge about their world. They want to do well, and then something goes very wrong.

The schools do contribute to the educational crisis that we have seen over the last several decades. Clearly, there are numerous factors contributing to the educational crisis, yet the hidden dangers discussed in this book compound the problems of all our youth, making school years more of a jail sentence than a magical time in the lives of our children. School years should be a time when children thrive, when they are full of life and so demonstrate an energy, a creativity, and a thirst for discovery. I did not write *Hidden Dangers* to place blame on any institution; I wrote it to make us aware of the often-overlooked problems within our educational system and to allow for changes to be made that help all students.

Hidden Dangers is a decidedly readable book that will be meaningful and helpful for all educators, psychologists, parents, coaches, and all those working with children. Even the students themselves may benefit from understanding that, indeed, the system may be part of the problem that they have been experiencing in school. This is not to say that students don't have responsibility for their learning — yes, they do. In fact, I suggest giving students more responsibility for their learning once all involved have a clear understanding of the dynamics of the hidden dangers.

Reader's Note

The stories of the children in *Hidden Dangers* are composites from listening and observing children who have experienced school problems over the years. Any resemblance between these cases and those of children you may know is unintentional. These stories are quite widespread in our schools and, indeed, show us that hidden dangers affect many children.

* * *

Portions of this book have appeared in other publications and are reprinted with permission:

"Toxic testing: It's time to reflect upon our current testing practices." *Educational Horizons, 83*(3), 212–220, forms the starting point for chapter 4 and parts included throughout the book.

"The new gender gap: Social, psychological, and educational perspectives." *Educational Horizons, 84*(2), 94–101, parts now incorporated in chapter 6 and throughout the book.

"Hidden dangers within our schools: What are these safety problems and how can we fix them?" *Educational Horizons, 83*(1), 66–76, forms the basis of chapter 7 and parts incorporated throughout the book.

Acknowledgments

So many people have been of help to me while writing *Hidden Dangers*. It is a book that has been brewing in my mind for some time; therefore, I am indebted to many people—educators, psychologists, parents, and students—who have contributed to its inception. I particularly want to acknowledge my former student, now graduate student, Nicole Sanborn, for her care and insightfulness in assisting with the interviewing of those who are experiencing hidden dangers.

I am thankful for Dr. Karen Erickson, dean of the School of Liberal Arts at Southern New Hampshire University. Dr. Erickson graciously helped find the time for me to complete this work. I also appreciate the efforts, skill, and patience of all those involved at Rowman & Littlefield Education. Their work has been a beacon of light guiding me to the fruition of this book.

Family and friends have played a significant role as well; their patience and unfaltering support helped to keep me on track with my writing. Dr. Michael Noonan deserves a special thank-you for his continued support and conversations about *Hidden Dangers*. And special thanks also to Tom Clarie for his careful and tireless proofreading skills.

One other note of thanks goes to my dogs, who stayed with me throughout the writing process in the wee hours of mornings and late into many evenings. They have been faithful companions throughout the writing process. One dear pet passed away after the completion of this book. She saw it through to the very end.

To all those involved, I offer my sincere gratitude.

CHAPTER 1

Understanding Hidden Dangers

If you are happy with the way things are in the schools, and your children are happy and fulfilled, fine. I'm glad you are happy, and the schools are doing what you want them to do for you. But there are lots of people out there who are very unhappy.

—John Holt

Why is it that so many children do not look forward to attending school once they are out of first grade? Why is learning a tedious process and not one full of joy for most children? I believe that we are having a crisis in our schools, unprecedented from those of other times in history. We are seeing more violence than ever before; more diagnoses of learning difficulties; more attention deficit hyperactivity disorder (ADHD) and other behavioral and emotional problems; and more concerns with students' not attaining basic skills in reading, writing, and mathematics and the skills needed for success in our technologically oriented society. Although we live in the richest nation on Earth, the academic achievement of our children is lagging well behind that of youth from many other countries around the world. This crisis is well known to informed government officials, educators, and parents alike. In 1983, the National Commission on Excellence in Education made the following statement:

The educational foundations of our society are presently being eroded by a rising tide of mediocrity that threatens our very future as a nation and as a people. . . . If an unfriendly foreign power had attempted to impose on America the mediocre educational performance that exists today, we might well have viewed it as an act of war. As it stands, we have allowed this to happen to ourselves. (quoted in IllinoisLoop.org, 2006b, para. 31)

There have been numerous educational reform attempts over the years to rectify the problems, including President Clinton's Goals 2000. The most recent nationwide effort involves the No Child Left Behind Act (NCLB), signed by President George W. Bush on January 8, 2002 (see U.S. Department of Education, 2004). Like previous educational reform acts, it was intended to improve schools — this time, by focusing on accountability, measuring student progress, utilizing proven educational methods, and allowing freedom for states and communities, as well as choices for parents. This mandate may look good on first glance, but it is contributing to our problematic conditions and exacerbating many of the difficulties experienced by children in our schools.

Although test results are showing some improvement for many students, these results come at a high cost of decreased depth of learning and lowered motivation. NCLB decreases the time that teachers have to work to help students develop critical and analytical thinking skills. Teachers must teach to the test, utilizing a testing format that many of our deepest and most creative students often do quite poorly on. NCLB is leaving many students behind, and it has not aided the educational pursuit of excellence in our schools as intended (see Rose, 2004).

Educational policies should not come down to a power struggle between political parties. Government policies have all attempted to improve our schools, but when we look back over the years, it appears that each incoming administration tends to undo the progress made by previous administrations. It is clearly time that we stop getting caught up in the politics of education and start looking at what is really happening in our schools. We need to hear from the experts who work most closely with children — the school administrators, school psychologists, counselors, teachers, and parents — and we need to hear from the children themselves. These are the true educational experts, who know the inner workings of their schools; these are the people who can make the difference if given the opportunity to challenge current ideas, policies, and practices.

After many years of working and volunteering in public and private school settings, interviewing clients in private practice, and teaching and researching at the graduate and undergraduate levels, I am concerned with what I am hearing from school administrators, clinicians, teachers, children, and their parents. Many "normal, typical" children are experiencing difficulties coping and learning in their traditional school settings. These children are our red flags alerting us to the fact that our schools are in serious trouble.

We need to take a clearheaded look at our schools and the problems that our youth are experiencing. We need to stop placing the blame outside of the schools and to start looking at the attitudes, beliefs, policies, and practices that guide our schools and the impact they have on each school's unique environment. By understanding the whole picture and the influence placed on each school's climate, we can make all schools places where children learn and like to be and where professionals can take pride in doing their best work.

What makes a superior school environment where children are safe, are learning the basics, and are challenged to their fullest potential? What possibly can be so original and work so successfully at some schools that students can hardly wait to get there, experience a sense of community and shared responsibility and receive an education that is broad and deep? Certainly, large public schools must address enormous problems, and most have limited financial resources to do so. However, it is possible for healthy conditions to occur in all schools, and although money can be helpful, it does not ensure an optimal learning environment.

So, how do we go about making the changes in our schools so that all children experience a sense of joy with learning? First, we must understand that what makes a school toxic to learning is a complex phenomenon to get your mind around. It's like trying to grasp a constantly moving ball of wiggling, slimy worms. One of the keys lies in understanding the school's climate.

School climate is not a new concept. It has been defined in a number of ways over the years. Originally, climate and environmental studies fell within the parameters of industrial/organizational psychology. However, over the last several decades, schools have become increasingly concerned with climate issues as more and more difficulties needed to be handled in the school setting. Halpin (1966) first described school climate and how one school varies from the next in atmosphere. He believes that each school has a unique "feel" and "personality" of its own and that open climates are the most beneficial (cited in Hoy, Tarter, & Bliss, 1990). Hoy and Woolfolk (1993) prefer a health metaphor. According to research conducted by Hoy, Tarter, & Bliss (1990) and Hoy, Tarter, & Kottkamp (1991), aspects of health tend to be a much better predictor of school effectiveness. We all know from our own experiences that each school has a unique feel or personality — some seem comfortable, safe, and thriving whereas others evoke feelings of anxiety. So what exactly do we mean when we talk of *school climate*?

Peterson and Skiba (2001) view school climate as a reflection of positive and negative feelings regarding the school environment that directly and indirectly affect a variety of learning outcomes. I choose to look even more broadly and define *school climate* as a unique combination of intellectual, behavioral, social, emotional, ethical, and physical characteristics of a setting that is highly influenced by the society in which it is located. I use the term *toxic* to refer to elements that interfere with learning and the general mission of the school. In contrast, the term *healthy* refers to elements that enhance learning and the general mission of the schools.

The climate of a school is easy enough to define, but it is a difficult and elusive phenomenon to identify. So let's take a close look at children who are exposed to toxic school conditions: typical students who are not thriving.[1] First up is Kevin.

Kevin is an 12-year-old boy from a family of two parents, both of whom work as professionals. He enjoys several close friendships with his classmates at school and with kids in his neighborhood. His interests include computer games, cars, and sports. Homework is a struggle, but once he gets started, he seems to complete the rather meaningless assignments without too much effort and thought.

Kevin sounds like a typical preadolescent child, yet he is one who scores well below average academically. He does not have a learning disability or any emotional and behavioral problems. To many parents and teachers, this scenario may sound quite familiar; it occurs frequently in the schools. However, because it is common, we should not assume that it is not a serious problem. When a child is not learning and becomes frustrated, angry, anxious, and depressed, it is a grave crisis, and the rest of the child's life is affected—and it's happening to more and more of our children.

What is going on? Why isn't Kevin living up to expectations? After all, he doesn't have any serious behavioral problems; on intelligence tests, he scores well above average; he has friends and a supportive caring family. At first, his parents blame him because it is he who is not achieving to expectation. But after some reflection, they realize that it may not be Kevin's fault. Kevin enjoys learning almost any subject that he has not been taught in school. He reads and writes well, although does not complete assignments for school. He is well behaved at home and at school, and he shows no signs of a passive-aggressive attitude or a desire to sabotage his learning. Kevin's parents and his teachers are puzzled by his lack of academic achievement.

His teachers, though well intentioned, react in a similar manner. They do not ask what might be wrong with their approaches to teaching, with their classrooms, with the school, and with the system. Rather, they immediately start looking for what is wrong with Kevin.

The school psychologist may be called in to test the child. Although the testing is geared toward finding strengths and weaknesses, the weaknesses are usually the focus for schools, and unfortunately, many adults put more faith in the results of testing than is warranted. Tests do not always show accurate results, for a variety of reasons, ones that I consider in a later chapter. However, with all the limitations of testing, of which there are many, comes a label and a diagnosis; oftentimes, these, too, are inaccurate. Once labeled, the child becomes the diagnosis (Noonan, M. A., personal communication, 2007). Teacher expectations change, and sadly, parental expectations change as well, and the child begins to doubt himself or herself.

Years of being misunderstood and poorly educated can easily lead to a variety of secondary psychological and learning difficulties, including anxiety, depression, frustration, boredom, bullying, violence, problems with self-esteem, poor academic achievement, and dropping out of school, to name just a few. All, however, represent the difficulties encountered by misunderstood children attending toxic schools. We can clearly see from the case of Kevin that he is an underserved child in a school setting that does not fit his needs — and he is definitely not alone.

Kevin's parents believe that their child has had several good teachers, but the teachers were limited in what they could accomplish because of the dysfunctional climate at each school. Many critics would say that these students and parents are seeing only the negative issues, that they don't understand the complexities of the schools, and that they are not objective because the problems involve their children. Indeed, this is a good point, but it is not always an accurate position to take. Fortunately for Kevin, his parents took his concerns seriously and did not overreact by looking for pathology where none existed. They simply changed his school setting, finding a much better fit for their child.

Kevin blossomed in his new educational setting. Additionally, he was able to keep his old friends while making several new ones. He also became confident in his work; indeed, he began to show the gifted side that his parents always knew was there but which previous teachers were not able to see. Kevin became motivated and was excited about learning; in fact, learning became his hobby, his life force.

There were no longer time boundaries to the school day. Learning continued to be exciting for Kevin throughout all waking hours of his day, late into the nights, and even on weekends. He was a kid who went from getting poor and, in some cases, failing grades to excelling with his studies. Kevin demonstrated an insatiable thirst for knowledge, for learning, for writing, and for being involved with helping others through experiential learning work. His parents no longer had to remind him to "buckle down" and start his homework. Instead, their comments changed to "Don't you think you've done enough? Come and watch a little TV with us" and "It's really time to turn off that computer."

Learning and life became an exciting adventure. Kevin is excited about his future; he's optimistic; and he is feeling safe and secure in his environment and with himself.

Although Kevin had to change schools to find an environment that was healthy for him, it is best to address the problems within the school's climate so that all children can thrive. Keep in mind that positive changes in school climate benefit all students, not just students who are showing symptoms.

In the next chapters, we will begin to discover why some schools have hidden dangers that interfere with optimal learning. Schools and classrooms vary greatly. One school may be producing students that are excelling and excited learners. Others, even those residing within the same school district and having the same policies, are experiencing student failure and increasing dropout rates. Furthermore, some schools may contain toxic and healthy conditions within the same building. The answers become clearer when we establish a solid foundation to understand children's basic needs, learning styles, and the need to foster and teach resilience, optimism, and flexibility.

> Most Americans have no idea how bad things really are. We are in a state of emergency. I'm blown away that this isn't what is on every parent's mind when it comes to elections . . . that people are not in the streets fighting for their kids.
>
> —Oprah Winfrey, regarding her special report *American Schools in Crisis* (quoted in IllinoisLoop.org, 2006c, para. 5)

NOTE

1. The cases in the book are composite sketches of children whom I have known and interviewed over the years. They are exemplary kids who portray the hidden issues involved with toxic schools, and I firmly believe that they represent the tip of the iceberg with regard to such issues.

CHAPTER 2

A Necessary Foundation
to Identify Hidden Dangers

Modern cynics and skeptics . . . see no harm in paying those to
whom they entrust the minds of their children a smaller wage
than is paid to those to whom they entrust the care of their
plumbing.

—John F. Kennedy

In many ways, it seems that we have not progressed too far from
these enlightened words of the 1960s. Teachers are still underpaid,
and although students have made progress in some areas, they have
lost ground in others. So let's take a closer look at the underlying issues. I firmly believe that it is essential to obtain all sides of the story
to fully comprehend a problem, but there is no need to reinvent the
wheel to understand the troubles in our schools today.

If we have a solid understanding of the research and work from
some of the best researchers and practitioners from the interdiscipli-
nary fields of psychology, education, and child health, as well as in-
sight into the mistakes of previous educational reform, including
those of No Child Left Behind (NCLB), we will have a firm foundation upon which we can begin to understand the hidden dangers
within our schools. Therefore, before I share my own work, I want
to apply the insights and research from several groundbreaking specialists in the fields of medicine, psychology, and education.

Boston Children's Hospital pediatrician T. Berry Brazelton and
child psychiatrist Stanley Greenspan have contributed greatly by
identifying the irreducible needs of children. We need to thoroughly
understand these needs and make sure that each is met in our
schools. According to Brazelton and Greenspan (2000), there are

seven such needs that every child must have in order to grow, learn, and flourish. Although their work was developed to express children's needs in all aspects of their lives, school clearly occupies a large part of most children's time, and many of these basic needs are not being met in our schools. These irreducible needs are as follows:

1. Every child needs ongoing, nurturing relationships.
2. Children need physical protection, safety, and regulation.
3. Children need experiences tailored to individual differences.
4. Children need developmentally appropriate experiences.
5. Children need limit setting, structure, and high but reasonable expectations.
6. Children need stable, supportive communities and cultural continuity.
7. Children need protection for the future while maintaining and supporting growth. (Brazelton & Greenspan, 2000)

At first glance these needs appear obvious, yet so many of them are not met for our children in our schools. These basic, irreducible needs should be the foundation on which we build our schools. However, I want to explain how these needs are being undermined. Let's begin with the first one. Certainly, children need primary caregivers, who are there for them for the long haul, but they also need committed teachers, who see their students through the school year and beyond and who are able to develop healthy, motivating relationships with them. Children also need committed administrators who are available to assist with parent, student, and community concerns.

Unquestionably, there are school personnel who are thoroughly committed to our children, and they do make a difference. But too many are there just to receive their paychecks, and many must hurry off to second jobs to make ends meet at home. Working with our children in the schools must be seen as one of the most important jobs in the world, second only to that of the parents.

Naturally, kids need physical protection, safety, and regulation, but are some of the practices in our schools undermining this need? I think the answer is a resounding *yes*. Since September 11, 2001, school policies have dramatically changed in an attempt to provide a safe environment. However, school lockdowns, metal detectors, and other such policies are making many children feel as though they are in constant danger.

Children also need safe, nontoxic buildings for health and learning. Unfortunately, many of our nation's schools are subpar on this issue because of the high cost of needed updating and repairs for problems involving asbestos, toxic molds, and other such hazards. Physical protection, safety, and regulation also mean that children need to be effectively protected from teasing, taunting, and disruptive behavior. As such, teachers should not be expected to cure, nor are they capable of helping, all children. Regular classroom teachers have not been trained to handle severe behaviorally and emotionally disturbed children, and ultimately, all children are put in a compromised situation. Children cannot learn successfully in settings where their basic need for protection is not met.

In applying the third need to our schools—that of experiences tailored to individual differences—we are aware that children need to feel respected for their individual areas of strength and weakness and that they need to have proper assistance to develop all areas to the fullest. Unfortunately, many schools are giving only lip service to this basic need. All children learn differently; understanding and flexibility are required. For example, during their early years, many children find it difficult to sit still. Blaming them and misdiagnosing them with attention deficit hyperactivity disorder (ADHD) is harmful. Such constant misunderstanding and awkwardness of fit with one's academic endeavors may lead to a self-defeating downward spiral resulting in lowered academic performance for both boys and girls. Some children, indeed, have ADHD and are in need of assistance, but far too many are diagnosed with this disorder than is statistically likely. Many in our schools really believe that individual differences are well addressed, but I believe that most schools do a poor job valuing the uniqueness of each individual and, in many cases, are actually harming the children's capacity to learn.

The fourth basic need (developmentally appropriate experiences) is another one that school staff and administrators believe is well addressed, but I beg to differ. All we need do is look at a typical first-grade classroom, where all children are expected to learn the same material at the same time. Because children develop at different ages, all are not ready to read or write or sit still at the same time. Educators need to meet them at their time. One child's brain might be developing with specific language skills whereas another one's seems to be excelling with spatial abilities. Educators must find ways of accomplishing developmentally appropriate tasks, inspiring children to learn, and allowing them to succeed (Connell & Gunzelmann, 2004). Children need to believe that they can accomplish life's tasks.

Children's need for limit setting, structure, and expectations is another area undermined in many schools. School rules must be clear, consistent, and reasonable, but they also must be flexible enough and allow each child to be responsible for his or her own learning. Our schools consistently get so hung up on problems of conduct that the main focus of education gets lost. As a result, many children across our nation do not understand that getting an education requires that they fully participate in the educational process. Children want to learn, and sparking that desire requires that we allow children to be responsible for their learning.

The need for stable, supportive communities and cultural continuity as applied to schools means that children need to feel that they are a part of their school communities. They need to feel a sense of belonging in terms of their unique gifts, cultural heritage, and individuality. Additionally, the schools need to fit in with the larger community. Unfortunately, many schools have a toxic environment: unfit for healthy relationships and dynamic learning.

The final basic need implies that all who are involved with children assist them with nurturing self-respect and self-acceptance, which is the first step for encouraging respect and tolerance for others. As educators, we need to begin by accepting each child, and we need to help them all become healthy, self-respecting individuals who value and respect the rights of all others, who see the need for differences, and who celebrate the diversity of others.

Although most of our schools today allow children of all races and nationalities to participate academically, I believe that the need for self-respect and tolerance of differences goes much deeper than ethnicity does. All too often, only lip service is given to this need in our schools. Rarely is true diversity genuinely celebrated: the respect and celebration of the creative uniqueness of every individual. Instead, the focus seems to be more on expecting children to be the same, to learn at the same rate and in the same manner, to behave the same way, and to not upset the apple cart with too many questions.

It seems clear that safe and productive schools must meet all the basic needs, and meeting these basic needs will benefit all individuals involved in our schools: students, teachers, administrators, staff, parents, and community members. Meeting these basic needs should be a starting point for all those interested in developing a positive school climate.

We also must learn from the mistakes of previous educational movements, including the self-esteem movement. To have esteem for one's self is a valuable attribute, but self-esteem cannot be given or taught to students. Self-esteem does not come from teachers' always praising the students but, instead, from the students' working hard and succeeding. False self-esteem, praising students when they know that they are not doing well, only helps to promote a lack of trying. Threatening children that they will not get into the college of their choice and that they will never get a decent job only makes kids give up in frustration. So much of what happens in schools in the name of trying to motivate students to do their best backfires and creates a climate of pessimism.

Martin Seligman (1995) offers a much more useful and hopeful approach to assisting students to understand and take responsibility for how they feel and think about themselves. Seligman sees self-esteem as a mental state, a way in which the child explains his or her successes and failures to himself or herself. If the child understands who is responsible, then she can be accountable for her own learning. If the child understands that there is something that he can do about his situation and that it will not have lifelong consequences, then the child can have an optimistic outlook, will be less apt to give up, and will be more likely to take responsible steps toward making his situation better. NCLB, with all its good intentions, is creating an atmosphere of evermore pessimism. The strong focus on accountability and test scores overlooks the needs of children, particularly, the needs to engage individual differences and developmentally appropriate programs.

We can learn a lot from Seligman (1998) about developing schools that are conducive to learning and are emotionally resilient. Seligman believes that we can and should teach our administrators, teachers, and students to be optimistic. If there is not an optimistic perspective present, failure can and will occur in school—even when talent and desire are present. Along with this, children must be taught the important life messages of not giving up and of mastering frustration and challenges.

Additionally, schools today are rushing children to grow up quicker, to comprehend concepts at earlier ages, and to behave as pint-size adults at the expense of their childhood. According to David Elkind (2001), this trend does not result in greater learning for the children, but it does put added stress on already overburdened children. Attempting to speed up children's learning can result in a weak academic foundation. Children do not understand many concepts at early ages. Therefore, material needs to be presented with a solid underlying foundation, which is all too often shaky when we hurry learning.

We also must consider the groundbreaking work of Dr. Howard Gardner (1999) and the applications that his theory has when applied to issues of school climate. Multiple intelligence theory can be quite helpful in establishing a nurturing, thriving, and safe school climate.

It looks at the following forms of intelligence: linguistic, logical–mathematical, musical, bodily–kinesthetic, spatial, interpersonal, intrapersonal, naturalistic, and existential–spiritual. We now know from school climate research that an optimal learning setting is one that understands, accepts, and respects individual needs and differences. By incorporating the theory of multiple intelligences and by viewing each child in terms of his or her unique intelligences, we are able to obtain a fuller understanding of the child and nurture each child's strengths while helping to develop areas that may be weak.

We also know that traditional intelligence tests do not show an adequate picture of an individual's intelligences. Furthermore, many children do not test well and are discriminated against as a result (we'll learn more about this in Chapter 4). We know from the research of Dr. Mel Levine (2002) that we must learn to celebrate the children for who they are and that different children are destined to bloom at different times in life when conditions are conducive for them to so. It appears that we are not yet fully addressing the needs of all individuals: We are seeing children with deficiencies that need to be fixed, rather than valuing the uniqueness of each child.

Now that we have established a solid footing for our foundation, let's take a closer look at how these cutting-edge researchers and practitioners help us to further our understanding of improving school climates. The viewpoints of Brazelton and Greenspan (2000), Levine (2002), Gardner (1991, 1999), and Seligman (1995, 1998), as discussed here, fit well with the six elements in my definition of school climate presented in Chapter 1. *School climate* refers to a balance of intellectual, behavioral, emotional, social, ethical/moral, and physical characteristics of a school.

INTELLECTUAL ELEMENT

Without question, academics need to be a major focus in the mission of all schools. However, schools with hidden dangers are overly focused on test scores, comparison and ranking of students, and a rigidity to learning. Safe, productive schools have high academic expectations for their students, observe individual learning styles, and focus on depth and application of learning. We know from the research of Levine (2002) that we must learn to celebrate the multiple intelligences of all children while respecting their individual needs for learning. Furthermore, Gardner (1999) and his multiple intelligence approach considers viewing each child's unique combination of intelligences as being much more respectful and less damaging to the child's self-concept than diagnosing. Children are not labeled or seen as being deficient but are valued for their uniqueness. Only then may students believe in themselves and understand that they can succeed academically.

BEHAVIORAL ELEMENT

All schools may experience problems of school disorder from time to time. School disorder includes issues of school violence, victimization, avoidance, perceptions of safety, and misconduct. According to Welsh (2000), research on school climate offers significant potential for understanding and preventing school violence. Issues of school disorder and violence are on the minds of most parents today and form a concern for many students as well. Yet, it is how these problems are handled that determines safe and productive conditions. In schools with hidden dangers, these issues may be handled with little regard for consistency. Bullying tactics may be inadvertently reinforced by attitudes that perceive the victims as being weak and in need of "toughening up"; problem students may be unintentionally given preferential treatment; and victimized students may not be heard with their silent cries for help. Additionally, living with the possibility of terrorist attacks and the heightened awareness of the volatile world events, students' perceptions of safety must be worked through. Furthermore, according to the research of McEvoy and Welker (2000), antisocial behavior must be viewed from a broad perspective and include research on academic failure and school climate. If we too narrowly focus on the individual as having the only problem, then ineffective interventions will continue. If, however, we begin to modify the climate where academic failure and antisocial behavior occur, then effective changes can take place and benefit all. In safe, productive schools, these same problems are present, yet the problems are faced head-on in an open, consistent, and fair manner. Teacher, staff, student, parent, and community concerns are genuinely heard and addressed.

EMOTIONAL ELEMENT

This element takes into consideration how those involved with schools feel about their schools and themselves. Are children and teachers feeling anxious, depressed, or pessimistic about their day-to-day work? Perhaps, their perspectives are contributing to these negative states. I certainly am not suggesting that schools alone are responsible for increased levels of anxiety and depressive disorders; what I am suggesting is that certain problems and issues can be approached differently in the schools to help develop a positive optimistic climate. We know from the research of Seligman (1998) that we can and should teach our administrators, teachers, and students to be optimistic. Again, according to Seligman, failure can and will occur in school if an optimistic perspective is not present, even when talent and desire are present.

SOCIAL ELEMENT

All schools develop a unique social aspect. In toxic schools, teachers, students, and parents may not feel as if they belong or as if they are valued and appreciated. There is little sense of community in such schools. In the best schools, a positive sense of community exists. Students, teachers, and administrators feel that they fit in and are making a positive contribution. It is not unusual to see older students helping younger students and accepting responsibility for the well-being of their schools and classmates. In safe, productive schools, there is a definite sense of belonging. Teacher, student, and parental input are all welcomed and seen as a genuine and valuable contribution.

ETHICAL/MORAL ELEMENT

This element can be determined by answering the question, are we doing good work? *Good work* is defined as involving excellence and ethics (Gardner, Csikszentmihalyi, & Damon, 2001). When excellence and ethics are in harmony, we can lead a personally fulfilling and socially rewarding life while doing good work.

Hoy and Woolfolk (1993) have studied teachers' sense of efficacy and its relationship to the organizational health of schools. They believe that teachers do not typically have the background and experience to handle day-to-day tasks in the classroom. According to the authors, inexperienced teachers—and even many experienced teachers—do not have a solid-enough grasp of psychological and learning theories to implement effective teacher–learning environments. Furthermore, teachers are asked to teach children with severe emotional, behavioral, physical, and learning disorders . Nowhere in their background have they been trained to handle these problems. Hoy and Woolfolk believe that beginning teachers must have additional coursework, time, support, and supervision to feel a positive sense of efficacy.

We also must ask other questions of ourselves: Are we doing the best we can for each child—adjusting to the uniqueness of each child, not looking for what is wrong but celebrating the strengths of the individual? In schools with hidden dangers, such questions are not readily asked. There appears to be a passivity on the part of those involved in the schools, and therefore, practices do not change. In the best schools, we see educators encouraged to question, to seek alternatives, to do their best work.

PHYSICAL ELEMENT

Last but certainly not least, we must consider the influence of the physical setting on the health of the school community. We have known from many years of teaching that the arrangement of desks, the colors of the walls, the size of the windows all have an impact on the climate of a setting.

More recently, we have become aware of research in the medical field that other factors may have an impact on health and ability to learn. These factors may include but are not limited to the food served in the cafeterias, undetected mold and environmental hazards that interfere with learning and the health of those exposed (see National Clearinghouse for Educational Facilities, 2007a, 2007b, 2007c). When students and teachers are continually exposed to conditions that are unhealthy, they are not able to do their best work. Indeed, many children's apparent hyperactivity, learning problems, and health issues may clear just by moving them to a physically healthy setting. It would certainly be unfortunate for such a child to suffer the consequences of misdiagnosis and needless medication when the building was the problem and all children, faculty, and staff would benefit by needed repairs and renovations.

A safe and productive school climate clearly involves a unique balance of the intellectual, behavioral, social, emotional, ethical/moral, and physical elements of a school. Addressing these basic elements will benefit all individuals involved in our schools: students, teachers, administrators, staff, parents, and community members and should be a starting point for all those interested in developing a positive school climate. Along with reviewing research, we must consult with teachers, administrators, pediatricians, school counselors, school nurses, community members, and, most important, the children and the parents. Doing so can lead to a more complete understanding of the school's total environment.

So, ask I did. Over many years, I have talked with teachers, doctors, administrators, school psychologists, school counselors, community members, and, of course, many parents and their children. I wanted to know what characteristics and conditions are believed to have caused problems for the children and what characteristics and conditions are important in order to have a healthy milieu. The answers are informative and go even deeper than the issues described in the brief case of Kevin. The information gathered gets at the heart of problems inherent in the hidden dangers within our schools and the essentials for developing thriving, safe school environments.

There are thousands of kids floundering in our schools and so not developing into the people whom they have the potential to become. Educating our children is our most important job as adults—helping them to become all that they are capable of becoming, to grow into the people whom they are meant to become. Yet, it seems that we are stifling the essence of our children and robbing them of the education they deserve.

The next several chapters look in-depth at the hidden dangers within our schools, ones that I have discovered from my work with educators, parents, and students and from being a parent myself. We begin in Chapter 3 by looking at the hidden danger of outdated and distorted attitudes, beliefs, and procedures.

> Teachers pass on the important information of the past and prepare their students for the future.
>
> —Gardner et al. (2001, p. 10)

Hidden Assumptions, Attitudes, and Procedures

More important than the curriculum is the question of methods
of teaching and the spirit in which the teaching is given.

—Bertrand Russell

Sometimes, the attitudes, beliefs, and procedures that have become
so ingrained in the schools just do not fit, explain, and help all children. There are many hidden assumptions, attitudes, and procedures
that routinely occur in schools without much thought and analysis.
One possible explanation is that we become comfortable with familiar routines, and we believe that we must be doing alright because
that's the way schools have always operated. Another likely possibility involves a combination of factors, including a lack of time, expertise, energy, and money to look thoughtfully into these issues, but
there definitely is a need to do so.

Let's begin by looking at issues within our society. No doubt, we
live in a wonderful country. However, having freedom and a right to
a free public education can have its shadow side. Possibly, we've
grown to expect that education is something that is given to our students, a passive process where many expect learning to be spoon-fed
to them. But a true education cannot be obtained in this manner. Education is a process that develops over time through hard work, dedication, and perseverance. It is undeniably a right for those living in
our country, but it is also a gift—a gift that must be earned. All too
often, we see students doing only the minimum of work to get by in
their classes. Our natural response is to blame them, to say that they
are lazy, unmotivated, even ungrateful. But they have learned these

behaviors from their parents, from their teachers, and from society. We cannot change this norm overnight, but we can make small changes within our schools to triumph over this self-defeating learned behavior. Change is a difficult and often slow process because of the significant resistance to change within many schools.

However, this resistance can be overcome if we acknowledge that there is a problem, stop blaming, and change what we can. Yes, I know that there are many problems in our society over which we have no control—poverty, violence, family issues, to name a few—but there are also hidden resistances in our schools that, if identified, we can do something about. One such hidden resistance involves the assumption that if a child is not learning, then there must be something wrong with him or her. So, why are we reluctant to consider the possibility that the child might not be to blame? Well, I suspect that it is the age-old issue of human nature. We all can become a bit defensive when we believe our work, our personhood, is being attacked. However, this is a huge misunderstanding of the issues at hand. We do not need to feel defensive when some children are doing reasonably well in our classes. We should instead be asking the question, "What can we do differently so that struggling children— so that all children—can do better?" Ideally, it is best to address the issues of any child from a holistic perspective, including a complete analysis of the school's climate. Keep in mind that positive change in school climate will benefit all students, making school a safer and more productive place for all. However, a holistic analysis is not what usually happens. More often than not, the struggling child is seen to have a problem that must be addressed, as opposed to the teachers asking what factors in the environment could possibly be interfering with the child's learning.

Resistance to change is natural; it is a part of our human nature. It is difficult to acknowledge that our beliefs, our policies, and the approaches that we've been educated and trained to use might not always be best. However, I believe that most of us in the fields of education and psychology want to help the children with whom we work. Therefore, it is of utmost importance that we be open-minded to the possibility that we need to question our policies and practices. We need to keep abreast of the current research in our fields, consult with professionals outside our fields, and acknowledge our limitations. We need to look at all possible factors that are contributing to the problems that we are seeing with our children in the schools.

Another hidden problem involves a faulty assumption based on a misinterpretation of research. One such example involves misguided efforts to help children develop positive self-esteem. The self-esteem movement noted in the previous chapter began in the late 1960s with a research project done by Stanley Coopersmith (1967, cited in Seligman, 1995), a project that was misunderstood. Coopersmith, a psychologist, believed that raising children's self-esteem was important in proper child rearing. His results correlated well with sage, old child-rearing practices that require clear rules and enforce limits for children to develop high self-esteem.

Unfortunately, many educators paid attention to only the feeling-good part of boosting the child's self-esteem, thus lavishing praise on children for their work, even when children knew that they weren't doing well and putting forth their best efforts. Clearly, this approach has backfired. Encouraging a false sense of self-esteem without putting in the hard work is a dangerous approach. Indeed, self-esteem decreases when children realize, as most of them do, that the praise they have received is unfounded.

Academic policies must be continually appraised and revised when needed. The case of Nathan portrays a good example of a problem that can occur from a misguided assumption. Nathan was in eighth grade and doing little reading at home, when his parents became concerned. Nathan was not a boy who liked to read for pleasure although he was surrounded by books at home and his parents were both ardent readers. They believed that the manner in which reading assignments were approached during school time, and definitely for homework, were contributing to Nathan's lack of reading for pleasure. Nathan explained that he was required to read 10 pages of a novel of his choice, then stop and write a journal entry about what he had read. This approach was counterproductive to really getting into a page-turner of a novel and not wanting to put the book down; it was disruptive to the joy of reading.

Nathan was not even close to doing his best work, but his teacher was nonetheless commending his petty effort. So, Nathan's parents asked the teacher what the assignment entailed. She reported that Nathan was correct in his understanding and that students were required to read only 70 pages over the course of the term. Now, how can anyone learn to love to read when expectations are so low and when one has to stop every 10 pages? No one is going to enjoy reading this way. Low expectations form a detrimental danger in undermining all students' unrealized abilities—abilities that may remain concealed in such an environment.

The teacher's explanation of this absurd approach was that she didn't want the children who were poorer readers to feel bad. Students could always read more than what was assigned, but Nathan, like most boys his age, took the easy route—and was being harmed by this poorly thought-out and dangerous process.

Then there is the case of Mark, which helps to illuminate other hidden ideas and policies in the schools. Mark is a 10-year-old child from a typical household. Mom and Dad both work outside the home, but Mom returns home at three o'clock in the afternoon to be available to her children. Mark has an older sister and one younger brother. He is active and engaged with learning in the classroom, and he gets along well with his classmates. After school, Mark likes to relax for a while, playing basketball in the driveway and riding his bike around the neighborhood. Like most boys his age, he likes computer games, sports, and watching television, although his parents limit the amount of time and the programs that he is allowed to watch.

Mom and Dad are caring, involved parents who place a clear value on education. This case study sounds like an ideal supportive family, and Mark sounds like a typical boy with strengths and talents in many areas. However, in school, Mark developed the reputation of a child with hyperactivity and attention problems. His teacher strongly suggested that the boy be put on Ritalin. Clearly, this teacher was overstepping her bounds, having no credentials to diagnose attention deficit hyperactivity disorder and suggest the use of medication. Although this diagnosis was ruled out by his pediatrician and a psychologist, the label stuck within his school. It seems that in some schools, there is an overabundance of children with a diagnosis—if not this diagnosis, then another—and children become what we label them.

Unfortunately, this is not an unusual scenario. Many children are viewed as being deficient or different because they learn differently, are not learning up to expectations, and are not behaving as most other children. Sometimes, an accurate diagnosis is helpful, but a misdiagnosis can be harmful. This mislabeling and misperception of the child is not done intentionally, but it frequently happens as a matter of routine, without looking at other possible causes, because the child may exhibit some characteristic symptoms of a disorder. Nevertheless, the misunderstanding and overuse of diagnosis can be at tremendous cost to the child.

The school's motives are almost always well intended: School personnel do not want to overlook a treatable problem. However, are we in turn overlooking other possible causes of school difficulties by simply labeling—that is, blaming—the child and undermining the child's security and sense of self, when changes within the school may be all that is necessary? There are so many inherent dangers with diagnosing that we will look in-depth at these issues in Chapter 5.

Then there is the case of Sally. This case helps to clarify four other hidden procedural problems that can be identified early and corrected if we look at and accurately understand the symptoms of children who are experiencing school-related anxiety. These hidden issues include a lack of continuity, undertrained personnel, toxic testing, and overscheduling.

Sally's parents reported that she was anxious in school. She got off to a difficult start in first grade, when her teacher went on maternity leave and there were several substitutes for the remainder of the school year. We know from Chapter 2 that continuity is important, particularly to young children (Brazelton & Greenspan, 2000). Could this be causing some of Sally's anxiety? A similar problem involves school systems when they are going through a redistricting process, another procedure that we should question. Some students are sent to a different school as a result, uprooted from friends and the comfortable familiarity of their previous neighborhood school, often paying a high emotional price for a policy based on anything but the child's needs.

By the second grade, Sally reported that she found it difficult to focus on her work; she was worrying what might happen next. There were two children with severe behavior problems in her class. At times, they threw chairs and other objects, and they even hit other students. Naturally, these students required a lot of extra time from the classroom teacher, who was not trained to handle behavioral problems of this proportion. Sally often sat under her desk when things got out of control in the classroom. Here is the hidden dilemma related to teachers' not having adequate training, expertise, and supervision to know how to handle children with severe emotional and behavioral problems. We certainly wouldn't allow a surgeon to operate without proper credentials and training, yet we are entrusting the education and, ultimately, the futures of our children to people who lack adequate expertise. Most teachers would welcome additional education and training. They want to help children, and they take their jobs seriously. For the most part, teachers are not the problem.

Of course, we should mention two serious problems at this point. We should be encouraging the best and brightest of our college students to become teachers. But many of our talented young adults want to go into fields where they can command higher salaries. Teachers are underpaid. Another problem involves the tenure policies that allow poor teachers to stay at their jobs, collect their paychecks, and rob children of the education they deserve. And we reward our best teachers by having them teach children who will learn anyway.

A quote from Hillary Clinton clearly articulates this problem:

Merit pay to individual teachers would discourage teachers from helping troubled students and would create a distorted competition among teachers. I don't think that's a very good way to inspire teachers. We want our best teachers to work with the kids who are the hardest to teach. If teachers are going to be told that the people who look better on a test are the ones who are going to get them rewarded in salary or compensation, why would anyone take on the kids who are harder to teach? (*New York Times*, April 6, 2000, p. 25)

Furthermore, we must question the policy of tenure. Currently, schools get stuck keeping teachers who have lost their enthusiasm and others who clearly are incompetent and not dedicated to their profession and, in some cases, even harmful to the learning process of children. Such teachers need to be given a chance to change and improve their approaches, but they should not be allowed to remain, negatively affecting the education of children year after year. Yes, it is important to have some degree of security in one's job, but there also needs to be the motivation and ability to consistently do good work. In such a positive school climate, both the teachers and the students benefit. Over time, our nation's schools have been expected to take on more roles and responsibilities. These additional tasks are ones for which classroom teachers have not been adequately prepared and fairly compensated. Teachers are expected to be the jack of all trades. Many school systems respond by putting a teacher's aide in the classroom. The aide is usually someone with little or no training. This response makes no sense at all and at best can only be seen as a Band-Aid approach to a serious problem.

By third grade, Sally was exhibiting other concerns related to performance anxiety. Third grade was the year that all students take standardized achievement tests, and her teacher was stressing the importance of these instruments. Testing has taken on far too much importance in our schools. The hidden dangers of testing need a chapter of their own and are analyzed in-depth in Chapter 4. Additionally, Sally was overscheduled with after-school programs, including drama, soccer, and music lessons (see *The Hurried Child*; Elkind, 2001). Yet, her school required her participation in many extended-day activities and graded her participation on her report card. There was even some required weekend participation. Sports, music, and other formerly relaxing activities became a competitive, compulsory grind.

Even looking at a typical day's academic schedule should get us thinking. Students are required to change subjects every 45–50 minutes (for younger children, even more often). The rationale behind this hectic schedule involves the idea that children cannot maintain attention for long periods, but this is an inaccurate belief and a faulty approach for many learners. They can easily get back to the tasks at hand and learn in more depth if they are not required to stop and change classes and subjects when they are engrossed in learning.

Arbitrary time restraints are ludicrous, and this includes times for lunch, bathroom breaks, and other basic needs. Kids should be allowed to address their basic needs when necessary. For example, it's difficult for many students to think in class right before lunch, when they haven't eaten since early morning. Even adults are allowed a coffee break midmorning.

In classes that end at the bell, students are anticipating this event and have long before shut down their learning. These barriers are disruptive to all students, particularly those who learn in-depth. Many students cannot turn off their thinking in one subject, then quickly gear up for art or history when still deep in thought about a math problem or a concept that sparked their interest in the previous class. It is wrong to interrupt this thought process.

We should look at some of the interpretations of the laws developed to protect the children's right to education. Terms like *least restrictive environment, mainstreaming,* and *inclusion* are meant to protect children from being discriminated against, thereby allowing children with special needs to be integrated into regular classrooms, which, of course, is a good idea—most of the time. But there are definitely times when a regular classroom cannot provide the education that some children require to "not be left behind."

Teachers cannot be experts in all areas, and we are doing a disservice by not placing students with those having expertise in dealing with specific issues. It may be best for a child who is experiencing severe learning difficulties to be placed in a specialized school for a year or two until the child can be taught in the manner in which he or she learns best. Then, the student can be integrated back into the mainstream, with self-esteem intact, and with skills to thrive academically. Also, teachers should be chosen for each child based on the child's needs, not which classroom has space.

Another idea might allow a parent to switch the child's class or school when there is a failure to thrive in an academic setting. Sometimes, just a change in school settings is all that is needed, if it is a change to a school with a better fit for the child. It's not unusual for a child to be receiving poor grades and experiencing numerous problems because of a school setting. The special education team may be called in, searching for problems (with the child, the parents, even society) when all that may be needed is a change in school environment.

Then there is the issue of the number of students in each class. Well-documented research clearly shows a correlation between smaller numbers and higher levels of achievement. Large classrooms require teachers to teach in different ways. It's much more difficult to conduct experiments, debates, and seminars with large classes. Lecture is the more typical approach, but it does not meet the needs of many students. In the early grades, teachers use many worksheets, sometimes to reinforce learned material but sometimes just as busywork to keep large classes under control.

Carol's story is a good example of the effects of this dysfunctional approach. She is an only child of an intact professional family. Carol began hating school by third grade; she continually complained that school was boring and that the work was the same, day after day.

According to Carol and her parents, there were far too many worksheets, and these were seen as an attempt to keep the children busy in a classroom with too many students, many of them with problems too difficult for the teacher to handle. Although there was a teacher's aide in the classroom, this aide had no educational background and training. Typical children were not thriving in this setting. Research backs up the premise that smaller classes do make a difference.

Homework is another area that needs to be looked into. Certainly, homework is necessary at times to reinforce learning that occurred during the day. However, it seems that more and more homework is being assigned because of arbitrary homework policies—for example, high school students should do 2 hours of homework each night. Such policies need to be revised. Most homework is only busywork, which frustrates and turns kids off to school. Time can be much better spent relaxing with family, reading a good book, and playing sports.

The age-old issue of grading, progress reports, and report cards is another policy that needs revamping. Students get far too much negative feedback, become anxious, and, worse yet, stop caring. Chad is a young student suffering from the ill effects of this policy. Chad's mother was sent weekly progress reports but noted that only negative comments were reported—never any positive comments even though Chad is a bright, academically successful child. Grades were intended to motivate students and inform them of their growth. Instead, they have become a form of punishment with all the harmful ramifications.

Discipline and behavior management issues are far too much of a problem for all schools. In fact, I believe that there is so much of a focus on what kids might do wrong that many kids are beginning to think that it is the norm to act in an inappropriate manner. Clearly, all teens do not act irresponsibly all of the time. Many teens do not experience regular periods of storm and stress, as the media seem to portray. We need to start expecting that children can and will act responsibly.

Along these same lines, children need to be given responsibility for their learning and have choices in what they want to learn and how they want to learn it. We need to trust that they want to learn, that they want to do the right thing, and that they will behave in their best interests—at least most of the time. Many of our current educational policies on discipline and behavior are counterproductive to the mission of the schools to teach children to become responsible, knowledgeable individuals. (Our new school safety policies are addressed in depth in Chapter 7.)

One parent expressed her concerns regarding the inflexibility of the manner in which students were handled when disciplinary issues did arise. She described her child's school as having only one way of dealing with problems, a very inflexible way: "[The administrators and teachers] have this pretense that the kids will sit quietly at their desks, do all of their work, and life's going to be perfect." That is, they don't allow for individual differences.

Another parent, the mother of David, expressed her thoughts about the poor handling of discipline problems. The school's policies were reported as being inconsistent and ineffective. For example, one boy was frequently out of control in the classroom, and there was an incident involving physical violence. The aggressive child was spoken to in the principal's office and then sent back to class with no other consequences or follow-up. There are numerous stories when serious discipline problems were not handled appropriately.

This same parent volunteered in the classroom and observed other problems. She expressed concern that the children who had obvious behavioral problems were being rewarded for their inappropriate actions. She noticed that in special classes, such as music and gym, these children were allowed to use the drums or their choice of musical instrument just so there wouldn't be an incident. She spoke of children with severe behavioral and emotional disorders who took all of the teachers' time and energy at the expense of the other children. The regular kids were being left out and falling through the cracks.

It also appears that in school settings, boys are in time-out and other forms of disciplinary measures much more often than girls. This phenomenon should get us wondering why this is the case. Are boys not ready for school? Do boys have more behavioral problems? Are there gender expectations in our schools that are not realistic? There are behavioral differences between the genders, and little boys should not be made to feel as if they are "bad" because they act differently than girls do. Girls usually have a much easier time with rules in the school setting. I'm not saying that we should overlook or excuse the inappropriate behavior of some boys, nor should we throw up our hands and give up, ranting the platitude "boys will be boys." But, possibly, we should understand boys better and change the school climate so that it is more conducive to them (Gunzelmann & Connell, 2006).

Then there are the issues involved with the *tone*, or attitudes, of the administration, faculty, and staff. In many schools, this tone is pleasant, welcoming, and affirming. However, there are schools where even the parents feel threatened, almost as if they are children themselves and have been called down to the principal's office. In such schools, communication is not welcomed, and parental involvement is not encouraged. These are closed schools where the attitudes are authoritarian and nondemocratic. There is no room for negotiation or reflection on the school's assumptions, attitudes, and procedures. One parent summed up her thoughts succinctly about such a setting: She believed that the tone was set by the upper administration, and if nothing was done, the problems would indeed perpetuate.

She understood that in her child's system, the superintendent backed up the principal, the principal backed up the teachers, and the teachers backed up the staff, but that there was no one to listen to the parents and the students. In the case of one child, Becky, emotional harm was caused by an unkind lunchroom staff woman, who spoke angrily and in a demeaning manner to the students. Becky was so fearful that she was not able to eat, and soon she and her friends skipped lunch altogether rather than encounter this paid bully. Bullies aren't always the kids. Unfortunately, no one listened to these children or to the parents. The personnel and policies remained.

We also must consider the timing of the school day. Research study after research study well documents that during adolescence, natural sleep cycles change so that teens stay awake later and thus need to sleep later in the morning (National Sleep Foundation, 2007). Unfortunately, most high schools start early; 7:30 a.m. or earlier is not unusual, which means that many adolescents are getting up by 5:30 or 6:00 a.m. to finish homework and get on the school bus. However, adolescents need at least 8 to 10 hours of sleep per night; otherwise, they run an increased risk of depression and having attention issues, along with a decrease in learning, not to mention a higher risk of car accidents for those sleepy students who have their driver's license. So what do the schools do? They start the academic day earlier and earlier—based not on research, which clearly states what is best for the child, but on a budget issue. School buses cost money, and the high school students must get up and start early so that the younger children can then be picked up and brought to their schools.

Even basic policies on eating and exercise need reviewing. Children need nutritious food, and they need it more often than adults. Many children need to eat several small healthy meals throughout the day. Yet, the school schedule does not allow for this need. According to the professionals at the Mayo Clinic (2006a), children, unlike adults, need extra nutrients and calories to fuel their growth and development. Many children are unable to focus, particularly in the class right before lunch, because their need for food is more urgent than anything the teacher might be attempting to teach. When children are allowed to pay attention to their bodies' needs, they learn to eat when necessary and not when they are not hungry. If children were allowed nutritious snacks during the morning hours, if and when needed, many children would be more alert and not crave the high-fat and sugary temptations that are the target of many in need of quick energy. Parents and educators should also be aware that food additives and colorings can interfere with sensitive children's ability to focus and learn. Because such additives do not have a nutritional value, they should be avoided by all children.

When lunchtime finally arrives, children typically have 20 to 25 minutes for lunch, which includes standing in line. Usually, there are only a few minutes to gulp down a few bites; the rest is dumped into the trash. Lunchtime needs to be relaxed, allowing time for socialization and a break from the academic routine. Nutritious selections must be all that is accessible for children, along with adequate time for consumption. Several tempting choices should be readily available, including healthy main courses and desserts. The incidence of childhood obesity has grown rapidly in this country for many reasons. We live in an industrialized nation where fast foods are a way of life for many, offering convenience, availability, and attraction to children through aggressive advertising campaigns. According to research from the Mayo Clinic (2006a), in just two decades the prevalence of overweight children has doubled in the United States for youth between the ages of 6 and 11. The obesity rate has tripled for American teenagers. Furthermore, the annual National Health and Nutrition Examination Survey by the Centers for Disease Control and Prevention found that about one third of U.S. children are overweight or at risk of becoming overweight. In totality, it appears that approximately 25 million U.S. children and adolescents are now considered overweight (cited in Mayo Clinic, 2006a).

Although there are some genetic causes for childhood obesity, most result from poor choices of food, too much food, and decrease in activity levels. Sedentary lifestyles are on the rise, and schools need to address the changing times. Clearly, technology has advanced the potential for educational attainment, and most kids enjoy and excel in the use of technology. Yet, it does decrease the amount of time that kids are engaged in active pursuits.

Amazingly enough, the trend in education has been to ignore this need for increased activity levels by cutting down on the required hours and days during which children must be involved in physical education. Particularly at the middle school and high school levels, adolescents are required to take only one term of physical education per year. Even in elementary school, recess times are few and far between because of the faulty belief that academic time is being wasted if kids are out running around. In truth, kids are able to focus better when their need for physical activity is addressed—particularly for kids who may be misdiagnosed as having attention problems. Even the physical layout of the school building and classrooms needs to be considered. The products used in building and in renovations and upkeep are problematic in many of our nation's schools. When new schools are being constructed, careful planning must go into the specifications and thus include information from architects and builders, along with research from the fields of education, psychology, and medicine to address these concerns. These issues warrant a chapter of their own and are so addressed in Chapter 8.

This chapter looks at serious issues involved with schools that are the most troublesome, where assumptions, attitudes, and procedures

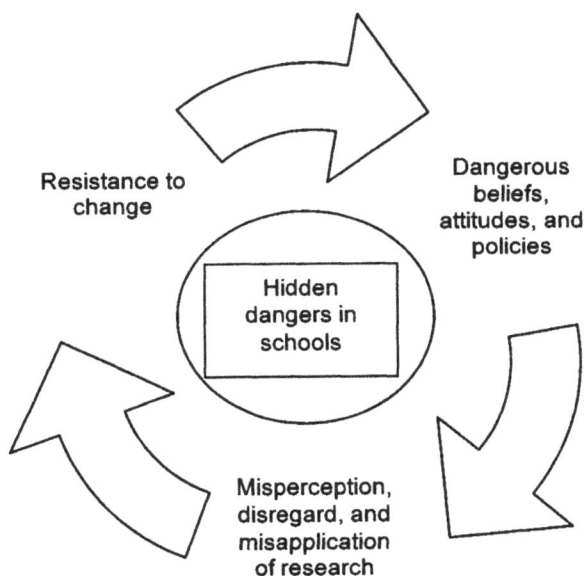

Figure 3.1.   Hidden-Dangers Vicious Cycle

are determined and implemented in the name of education. Many other countries do not have the same issues in their schools. We need to ask ourselves why so many of our children do not want to go to school, why they do not value a good education. Even those who do manage to graduate from high school are often ill-prepared to deal with the academic rigor they encounter when attending college.

It has not always been this way in our country, and we can make changes to improve the quality of education before more harm is done. We'll see all of these hidden themes emerge again in a variety of circumstances and cases as we look in-depth at hidden dangers. It is helpful to keep the *hidden-dangers vicious cycle* (see Figure 3.1) in mind as we go through the following chapters.

> It is, in fact, nothing short of a miracle that the modern methods of instruction have not yet entirely strangled the holy curiosity of inquiry; for this delicate little plant, aside from stimulation, stands mainly in need of freedom; without this it goes to wrack and ruin without fail. It is a grave mistake to think that the enjoyment of seeing and searching can be promoted by means of coercion and a sense of duty.
>
> —Albert Einstein

CHAPTER 4

Hidden Dangers in Testing

Our students are tested to an extent that is unprecedented in American history and unparalleled anywhere in the world. Politicians and businesspeople, determined to get tough with students and teachers, have increased the pressure to raise standardized test scores. Unfortunately, the effort to do so typically comes at the expense of more meaningful forms of learning.

—Alfie Kohn

My reason for writing this chapter on hidden dangers of testing began back in my early undergraduate years when a college professor from the field of educational psychology disclosed his personal history. When he was in kindergarten, he had been administered an intelligence test on which he performed quite poorly. Because of the test results, he was placed in a residential school for the mentally retarded. One young woman recognized after some time that he was not quite like the others; indeed, he seemed to be quite bright. Fortunately for him, this woman was able to get him out of the institution and back into a regular school, where he thrived. This young boy grew up and went to Harvard University, from which he received his doctoral degree.

Well, one might say that this was many years ago and could never happen today. Unfortunately, we are still harming children with the effects of toxic testing in our schools. Our schools are caught up in a testing obsession that has its roots in the accountability movement of earlier decades. Don't get me wrong, being accountable is a good thing, and student learning should be measured and documented, but how we are determining a student's learning is the problem. We're putting too much confidence into tests, and the scores are interpreted as an accurate reflection of a student's knowledge, skills, and abilities. Many students do not perform well on certain types of tests.

Testing in and of itself is a neutral process; it is when testing is misused that it can become a dangerous process. I have been involved with assessing students' learning for many years now. Earlier in my career, I was involved with diagnosing students with learning disabilities and other disorders. After years of using tests to measure, diagnose, and establish appropriate educational plans, I have done a 180-degree turn in my viewpoint on the usefulness and effectiveness of many traditional tests. In fact, I see many assessment approaches as being imprecise and even damaging for many students.

Scott is one such student who was misunderstood on numerous school assessment instruments. He is an easygoing 13-year-old who is a delight but has oftentimes been a puzzle to his parents and teachers. He is a conscientious student who overall still likes school. He did well on classroom work and easily followed the lectures and activities, although at times he got teachers off track with his insatiable curiosity and unique spin on classroom discussions. He seems to know a lot about many subjects and is inquisitive about most topics.

Scott has a few close friends, no diagnosed learning difficulties, and several intense interests. Math, science, foreign languages, and history are his favorites. So what is the problem one might ask? Well, Scott is one of those bright, creative students who do poorly on standardized multiple-choice tests, despite good grades and accelerated classes.

Students like Scott are plentiful in our schools; many students know more than they are able to demonstrate on traditional tests. A one-size-fits-all approach to testing is doomed to failure because of numerous imbedded problems with our current approach. To get to a fuller understanding of the hidden testing dilemmas, we need to step back in time and briefly look at historical precedents in the fields of psychology and education.

HISTORICAL PERSPECTIVE

Testing and evaluation procedures have been a part of educated society for hundreds of years, and individual abilities have been recognized since the dawn of history. The first tests were designed by the ancient Chinese around 2200 BCE. Plato and Aristotle wrote on individual differences as far back as 2,500 years ago. Many of the earliest tests included oral examinations and were presented with the biases unique to this approach (Aiken, 2000).

By the late 1800s and early 1900s, testing was beginning to take on a prominent role in the general public. In 1904, Alfred Binet was asked to develop the first intelligence test, to weed out children who would not benefit from traditional schools in Paris, France (Aiken, 2000). Thus, one of the first credible intelligence tests was born, although Binet was fully aware of the fallibility of the test scores. Certainly, this approach does not meet our needs today, where all children are entitled to an education, but such tests are still in use in revised versions, although scores may be no more accurate or useful than those of a century ago.

We must also understand that early psychological theory was closely related to philosophy and understanding the world through a qualitative methodological approach. Understanding the experience was essential, but during the late 1800s in Germany, Wilhelm Wundt started the ball rolling toward developing research approaches that would allow for quantifiable results. Measuring results became the theme for the next century and has continued into current times, and doing so is a good idea when used wisely. *Proper assessment* means using both qualitative and quantitative methodologies to fully understand the phenomenon being considered.

However, the field was moving quickly ahead, caught up in a trend of obsessively quantifying results without maintaining the more subjective (and at times deeper) understanding of the phenomenon being studied. In the United States during the late 1940s and 1950s, psychology was swept up in the behavioral era. B. F. Skinner and numerous other psychologists and educators were overinvolved in the desire to make everything measurable. Unfortunately, the outcome was that people put more credence into these numbers than was healthy and they forgot about the importance of measuring both qualitatively and quantitatively.

Significant historical and political developments brought about change in testing needs. For example, both World War I and World War II caused an increased need for innovative approaches to test many recruits in a short period. Then came the race to get the first man into space and the first man onto the moon, which had a domino effect resulting in a frenzied attempt to increase student learning in math and science. One might mark this as the beginning of an academic Olympics between the industrialized countries of the world. Thus, the big business of testing was born, along with an increased fervor for competition in academics.

These earlier attempts at testing seem to have established a mold that has been difficult to break. The pattern appears to address the style needs and thinking strategies of many students, but it does not adequately address the needs of all. In fact, I think it is fair to question whether we are accurately measuring the true abilities of any student.

TODAY'S PERSPECTIVE

Psychologists and educators know that it is wrong to make decisions based on a single test score. Decisions should be based on a balanced, complete understanding of each child. Numbers and scores can be misleading if we don't consider the whole picture, which means using both qualitative and quantitative approaches. Yet, because of economic, time, and political pressures, psychologists and educators are forced to rely more and more heavily on quantitative methods, and many have been deceived into believing that numbers tell the whole story.

Across the country, we have a continued movement toward accountability, increased use of standardized tests, and high-stakes testing. Along with these trends come the negative symptoms of teaching to the test, test anxiety, lowered self-esteem, misunderstandings of children, and missed opportunities for many. Elkind (2001) believes that our current testing obsession is a factor behind the dynamics of our hurrying schools. Administrators are under pressure to demonstrate student learning and are therefore teaching concepts at earlier and earlier ages. Doing so results not in greater knowledge but in added pressure for our children to measure up and to hurry up their learning.

Few countries in the world use standardized testing with children before the age of 16. But in the United States, we use such tests with young children even though we know that doing so is contradictory to research findings and recommendations. Furthermore, few countries use multiple-choice formats with any aged child (Kohn, 2000; see also, Kohn, 2004). Deborah Meier (2002) believes that this increase in the use of standardized tests undermines student achievement and increases the distrust that many have for teachers, students, and their own judgments. Parents may believe that teachers will see their children as less capable based upon faulty test scores, and students may doubt their own abilities by putting too much faith into the results of standardized tests that often do not show accurate proficiency. The misunderstanding of testing develops into toxic conditions for everyone who is affected by test scores: students, teachers, parents, administrators, and those in the entire school system and community. We know from research that there is no one test that can determine a student's ability or achievement. Nor is there a test that can measure a teacher's or a school system's effectiveness. To use tests in this manner is a flagrant misuse of testing, yet this is exactly what is happening.

Much of this drive toward accountability is fueled by political platforms. However, our well-meaning politicians are not trained in the art and science of testing, and many are influenced by the huge testing industry. Our children's education is too important to leave assessment decisions in the hands of those who do not comprehend the underlying issues in accurate assessment.

PROBLEMS WITH TRADITIONAL TESTING

Traditional tests attempt to show what a child does not know or what is wrong or deficient with his or her abilities rather than what is valued and unique about the child's particular way of learning, coping, reasoning, and problem solving. Test developers are looking at assessment too narrowly. We need to break out of the mold of traditional assessment and develop assessment procedures that value and demonstrate the uniqueness of each individual.

Traditional testing is at best a selection of test items that may or may not be relevant to the curriculum to which the student has been exposed, and it is always subject to many forms of bias, including cultural, gender, socioeconomic, and learning preference bias. Bias leads to assessment discrimination against many students, including bright, creative, deep thinkers; students with learning differences; students with a preferred learning modality; boys, because of gender differences; students from various ethnic and cultural backgrounds; and many students from lower socioeconomic backgrounds. This is a lot of children.

So with all these children at risk, why are we so reliant on traditional testing approaches? Well, as I stated earlier, testing is a big industry, and the testing manuals advertise questionable advantages. For example, traditional standardized testing allows for standard practices and scoring—that is, the tests are given to all students in the same manner and are scored the same way. But standardizing the process does not get rid of subjectivity. We are still making judgments, but in the case of most standardized testing instruments, we are making judgments on the lives of individuals, and we are doing so with little information. This results in a dangerous situation for many students.

Standardized testing also allows for a comparison of students. However, when students are ranked, the process ensures that half will be below average and that the uniqueness of each student will not be seen. Such practices give a false illusion of being scientific. Yet, we know from the work of Brazelton and Greenspan (2000) that for children to learn and thrive, we must meet their individual needs. We are not addressing individual needs with a one-size-fits-all approach to testing. There are many children with learning difficulties or just learning style differences, and most teachers do a good job of addressing these preferences in their teaching. But then we ignore the individual needs of most children when it comes to testing. We expect all children to be able to perform using one format. This is testing preference discrimination. Students should be allowed to demonstrate their competence in a way that shows what they really know and what they are capable of doing, while allowing their unique and often hidden abilities to shine through.

So with our current assessment strategies, kids like Scott, with unique, idiosyncratic responses to test items, are penalized. Their creative and deep-thinking approaches can actually handicap them on standardized tests. For example, a bright student may come up with answers that may be correct but are not the ones that the test designers had in mind.

Alfie Kohn (2000) gets this point across succinctly. He believes there is a correlation between high scores on standardized tests and relatively shallow thinking and that these kinds of tests are geared to a different, less sophisticated kind of knowledge. Kohn writes,

> There are plenty of kids who think deeply and score well on tests. There are also plenty of students who do neither. But as a rule, good standardized test results are more likely to go hand in hand with a shallow approach to learning rather than with deep understanding. (p. 10)

Meier (2002) concurs that deeper and more subtle thought is an impediment to scoring high on such tests. Meier and Kohn are not alone in their beliefs about deep thinkers. Even back in 1962, Banesh Hoffman, in the classic work *The Tyranny of Testing*, demonstrates that these tests penalize the finer mind:

> [The deep thinker] would see more in a question than his superficial competitors would ever dream was in it, and would expend more time and mental energy than they in answering it. That is the way his mind works. That is, indeed, his special merit. But the multiple choice tests are concerned solely with the candidates choice of answer, not with his reason for his choice. Thus they ignore the elusive yet crucial thing we call quality. (p. 99)

Furthermore, Hoffman states, "Multiple choice format also penalizes the creative student. Students who can imagine several possible correct answers, and may think the most obvious answer could not be the correct answer" (p. 101).

One renowned psychologist remembers back to when he was a young child and suffered from the harmful effects of testing. Dr. Sternberg states,

> I did poorly on the tests and so, in the first three years of school, I had teachers who thought I was stupid and when people think you're stupid, they have low expectations for you. . . . But my concern, given the relatively low predictability of the tests is that there may be people who have tremendous talents, creative and practical talents, who, because they don't do well on these tests, never get the chance to show what they really could do in important jobs. (quoted in BrainyQuote.com, 2007, paras. 7–8)

Differences among socioeconomic levels and race have been well documented in the literature for having an effect on test scores. However, there are less well-known issues of gender that influence standardized test scores. Dr. William Pollack (1998) believes that most of our schools fail boys when such schools do not have an environment that is conducive to the way that boys learn. Many schools do not have such an environment, and we are seeing a decline in boys' test scores as a result. Boys are often at a disadvantage on standardized multiple-choice format tests, particularly in the early grades, because of subtle wording differences between items. Girls definitely have an advantage here.

W. J. Popham (1999) believes that educational quality is being measured by the wrong yardstick, and therefore, the evaluations are apt to be in error. He also believes that most educators, as well as most parents, do not really understand the fact that standardized tests provide misleading estimates of learning and a school's effectiveness. Many of these tests are being used for high-stakes decisions, including student promotion and retention in grades, graduation, acceptance into certain schools, as well as judgments and punishments for the teacher—purposes for which the tests were not designed and which they cannot really assess.

All this—from tests that we know unfairly discriminate against a variety of students—shows only a limited sample of behavior, presumes similarity of educational content across classrooms, ignores individualizing ideas such as progressivism and constructivism, makes teachers and administrators narrow their curricula to the test content, and requires teachers to focus on test-taking skills, thus losing valuable instruction time. Furthermore, we are wasting taxpayers' money on these tests, rather than using needed funds for educational materials that would enrich all students. And most important, we are not getting an accurate picture of many of our students who may suffer humiliation and serious consequences from low scores.

It puzzles me how we can live in the most liberal country on Earth, where the rights of the individual are prized and protected, yet with our approach to educational testing, we expect everyone to demonstrate learning in the same way. Because students are all individuals with different achievements, different learning styles, different backgrounds, and different response styles, we must have a variety of testing formats if test takers are to accurately demonstrate their learning. We cannot tolerate a one-size-fits-all approach. Of course, we need high educational standards, but we need to be reflective about our purposes for testing. Such purposes might include the need to pinpoint learning problems to design appropriate educational programs, to improve the learning of all students, and to demonstrate that the children in our classrooms and schools are learning. To accomplish this goal of testing, we need to develop accurate assessment tools that do not have dangerous side effects.

We are definitely overusing and misusing a fallible method of assessment by relying on traditional standardized approaches. We can no longer afford to have such blind trust in a limited repertoire of assessment approaches. To break out of our current obsessive pattern of testing, we need innovative, motivated thinkers who know children well and realize the limitations of traditional tests, who are able to develop and fine-tune approaches that will measure learning over time, not just take a snapshot of a behavior.

> I'm glad that the real world doesn't come with built-in multiple choice boxes, precoded and ready to score.
>
> —Meier (2002, p. 181)

TOWARD A CONSTRUCTIVE SOLUTION

There are many ways to authentically portray each child's distinctiveness. Alternative assessment approaches can portray each student's unique abilities and learning styles. For example, many teachers have been using a form of portfolio assessment for some time—some more effectively than others. It can be a time-consuming process, yet it has the added benefit of helping students to take both responsibility for their learning and pride in their accomplishments.

Used well, portfolio assessment can demonstrate students' learning as well as their strengths and weaknesses, and it can help to determine an appropriate learning program for each student, not just for a few identified students. With further refinement, this approach, as well as other qualitative and quantitative approaches combined, could be used to compare students' abilities and to demonstrate the effectiveness of teachers' and educational programs' performance as well. Teachers will no longer be teaching to the tests but looking toward what other, more ethical approaches to teaching and learning might benefit each child.

CASE STUDIES

Case studies can help illuminate these ideas. For example, the case of Noel is excellent to demonstrate the power of portfolio assessment. Noel experienced difficulty in early grades. Reading and writing did not come easily. She was diagnosed with a learning disability during third grade and was functioning below her peers in language arts despite high intelligence scores. Traditional tests did help to identify Noel's weaknesses but were harmful to her in the manner that they were used — namely, because her program focused on remediating her weaknesses and did not shore up her numerous areas of academic talent. Her educational plan focused on the negative and did not allow the full child to develop. This was dangerous. Noel began to think of herself as being less smart than her peers; her self-esteem and self-confidence began to erode.

Test after test, year after year, her scores showed only her weaknesses. Noel developed a pessimistic outlook toward her future and felt trapped by a misleading approach to understanding her knowledge and skills. It wasn't until Noel reached college that she finally began to understand her strengths and to value her abilities. Through portfolio assessment, she demonstrated academic skills to herself as well as her professors. She became a confident and competent young woman, graduating from college with honors, and is now attending graduate school.

Noel was unique because she didn't give up. I suspect that many individuals have not persevered after test scores have put roadblocks in their way. The current high school dropout statistics are alarming to say the least. What a waste it is when human potential goes unrecognized or, even more sadly, is misunderstood.

Then there is the case of Suzie. Suzie was always an excellent student who performed well on all standardized tests administered throughout her elementary and secondary school years. While in college, she continued on this path toward success, clearly demonstrating her abilities as a scholar and an athlete. Yet, with all the praise and glory, Suzie had been too narrowly focused on scores and competition. She did not understand all of her strengths, which are numerous.

So, even in Suzie's case, we did not get a complete picture of who this young woman might become.

When Suzie became involved with an evaluation process that required her to focus on her strengths and weaknesses, likes and dislikes, she discovered new talents and a balance to her life, allowing more focused goals to emerge. Suzie was involved with experiential learning in her chosen field, trying out her knowledge and skills. This approach allowed for outside objective professionals, as well as her professors, to evaluate her abilities. Suzie took responsibility for her learning and discovered artistic talents, strong interpersonal skills, and a desire and ability to help others. Clearly, by only focusing on scores, ranking each student, and determining what a child does not know, tests too easily lose sight of the individual and his or her potential. Portfolio assessment is just one approach that we should seriously be looking at for use with all students, not just the severely handicapped, as is currently the practice.

To summarize, children are taught that the purpose of testing is to help them to review, to learn material thoroughly, and to show them what they still need to study—not to change options for their entire futures. Teachers need to use testing to see what information they need to readdress with students and how to modify their teaching approaches accordingly. Testing should not be used to harm students and teachers. To misuse tests in such a manner quickly establishes a toxic and dangerous climate.

> So the question, for me, isn't if we ought to have "standards" in our children's education. It is, rather, how and where they are determined, and by whom, and how they're introduced, and how we treat or penalize (or threaten, or abuse) the child or teacher who won't swallow them.
>
> —Jonathan Kozol (2000, p. x)

CHAPTER 5

Hidden Dangers With Labeling

There is a brilliant child locked inside every student.

—Marva Collins

Marva Collins founded the Westside Preparatory School back in 1975 in the inner city of Chicago. Children were admitted to this school who had been labeled as problem children, learning disabled, and, in the case of one child, borderline mentally retarded. After only one academic year, each student scored at least five grades higher, proving that the previous labels placed on them were inaccurate. Westside's graduates have gone on to many prestigious colleges and universities, including Harvard, Yale, and Stanford. These students are now professionals working as doctors, lawyers, and educators (Collins, 1996).

Unfortunately, the more common scenario for children who are labeled or, in some cases, misdiagnosed involves their not having an opportunity to be understood and to be allowed to develop to their fullest potential. Instead, their potential gets crushed by the very labels that are supposed to help them.

Remember Kevin, whom we met in Chapter 1? He is a 12-year-old preadolescent of at least above-average intellectual ability, yet his school grades do not reflect his academic gifts. He wants to do well in school but does not complete assignments, study for exams, and ask for help when he needs it. So what's going on with Kevin? Is he an unmotivated young man, possibly suffering from attention deficit hyperactivity disorder (ADHD) or from being learning disabled? What often happens in the schools is that professionals look to see what is wrong with the child who is not learning up to expectations and not at what might be wrong with the system, approach, teacher, and classroom climate.

Unfortunately, this is not an unusual scenario. Many children are viewed as being deficient or different because they learn differently, are not learning up to expectations, and are not behaving as most other children do. Sometimes, a child might indeed have a learning disability or other issue that interferes with learning, one that is in need of intervention. An accurate diagnosis can be an essential step toward getting the child the help that he or she needs. As such, labeling can be helpful at times, but oftentimes, children are overdiagnosed, misdiagnosed, and misunderstood, which is harmful.

This mislabeling and misperception of the child is not done on an intentional basis but frequently happens as a matter of routine without looking at other possible causes, because the child may exhibit some characteristic symptoms of a disorder. However, the misunderstanding and overuse of diagnosis can be at tremendous cost to the child. The school's purpose is almost always well intended. School personnel do not want to overlook a treatable problem, but are they in turn overlooking other possible causes of school difficulties by simply labeling the child? Furthermore, are some educational professionals overstepping their levels of expertise when suggesting that a child has a disorder?

These questions stuck in my mind as I sought to discover possible causes of Kevin's so-called attention difficulties. Many children do have true ADHD, but this diagnosis is being overused to label and treat children who are experiencing problems unrelated to a neurological difference. So, let's take a closer look at Kevin. Kevin's parents report that he was anxious in school. Like Sally from Chapter 3, Kevin got off to a difficult start in first grade when the teacher went on maternity leave and there were several substitutes for the remainder of the school year. Again, we know that continuity is important, particularly to young children (Brazelton & Greenspan, 2000). Could this have been causing some of Kevin's anxiety and increased activity level?

Kevin's mother was sent weekly progress reports during second grade but noted that only negative comments were made, although Kevin is a bright, academically successful child. Kevin needed to move around in his chair and periodically get up and walk around the classroom. Although this was against classroom rules, it is clear that many boys need this type of flexibility and freedom from time to time. Unfortunately, Kevin was beginning to develop a negative self-concept and did not enjoy going to school.

By third grade, Kevin reported that he found it difficult to focus on his own work. There were children with severe behavior problems in his class, and these students naturally required a lot of extra time from the classroom teacher. Kevin reported feeling not well cared for in this setting, and he experienced difficulty paying attention in school but not at home or elsewhere. Kevin's pediatrician helped rule out ADHD. Certainly, this was not a neurological problem but one involving a child who was aware that things were not quite right in his classroom. Instead of labeling Kevin, we could say that he was demonstrating an adaptive response to cope in a setting that did not meet his needs. He was clearly aware that all was not well in his classroom.

Kevin might also be considered a child who is a high reactor, or if we wanted to, we could diagnose him as having an anxiety disorder or some other disorder. But would this be helpful or harmful? I believe that it would be harmful to Kevin. The term *high reactor* is really just another label for characteristics that we should be valuing, not looking at as forming a disorder. Kevin was born with an innate love of life, laughter, and creativity. Right from the beginning, it was obvious to his parents that he was an unusual child; he was more alert, more aware, and indeed more sensitive than most infants. Laughter came easily and early to this robust child. He enjoyed everything about the world, finding humor in most situations, and he was interested in learning about everything.

Language, too, was an early gift. It appeared to be a central force for Kevin to be able to communicate his thoughts and feelings to others and to be able to connect with them in meaningful ways. His creativity, playfulness, and love of life often made him a handful to watch over. No doubt, he could get into more mischief than most kids his age, but he was never a problem for his parents. He learned the household rules easily and, most of the time, would abide by them. What happens to these wonderful qualities of curiosity, playfulness, creativity, and an eagerness to learn when children go to school? These traits are suppressed, and after a few years, all but disappear because we try to make children be the same, stay in their seats, color within the lines, be ready to read by first grade, and so on, as they progress through the school years. And if they are not ready or do not behave as we expect, then there seems to be a need to label them, to look for what might be wrong with them.

No doubt, Kevin can be a handful. Temperamentally, these so-called high reactors are interested more in their environment and may need more assistance from their primary caregivers and teachers to settle down. Oftentimes, these children are said to have difficult temperaments, but they should not be labeled *disordered*. These children are simply within a wide band of the normal range and are showing their unique colors. But might these characteristics also be considered an advantage? I think that the answer to this question is a resounding *yes*, as long as we do not try to label these kids as having problems. In fact, I would like to rename this temperamental category to that of *highly involved* children.

Kevin's parents had observed his classroom on several occasions and knew their son well. They decided to enroll him in a nearby private school, in hopes that he would experience a better fit. Since changing schools, Kevin is doing very well. He enjoys school, feels safe, is more challenged academically, and is allowed to move around when necessary. There has been no question of ADHD or any other problems at his new school. Certainly, the smaller number of children in the classroom helps, but that is not the only factor. The current school is described as being more flexible, and school personnel deal with problems immediately, taking the time to teach

each child to respect other students. Differences are seen as strengths, not weaknesses. Kevin is allowed to be himself and is accepted as a productive and valued member of his community.

Now let's look at the other side of the coin. A diagnosis or a label can have benefits because it can allow a child to have access to programs and to receive professional expertise not otherwise available. Certainly, if a child is having difficulty because of a primary neurological or psychological disability, it can be helpful to have the correct assessment so that the most appropriate treatment can then be obtained.

However, it is not as simple with learning disabilities and other diagnostic categories used in the schools as it might be if the child were diagnosed with strep throat and could then be prescribed the needed antibiotic. Learning disabilities, ADHD, autism, mental retardation, and any other diagnoses that schools must deal with are quite different. First of all, these diagnoses do not go away with time. Once the students are diagnosed, the labels stick with them throughout their school years and beyond. The children become the diagnoses.

Teachers often begin to expect less of these children because of their so-called disability. Even more sadly, parents may start to look at the child differently, and the child's opinion of himself or herself changes to one who needs help, who is different or inadequate in some essential way, thus clearly damaging his or her identity. The label lasts a lifetime, and these kids are being shortchanged from becoming who they were meant to be — all because of a label based on someone's assessment, which is oftentimes incorrect.

Furthermore, as used in education, the label does not determine the appropriate approach, program, or intervention to use with the child. There are numerous treatments and approaches to use with children who are diagnosed with any of the disorders in which schools must intervene. No one method is the best for learning disabilities, autism, mental retardation, or any other disorder labeled on a child. Each child must be assisted individually to find the way that he or she learns best, which can all be done without labeling the child. Indeed, this is how all children should be taught.

Additionally, educational interventions should be available for all children. We should not make it necessary for a child to be labeled to get the services that he or she needs. All children should have access to whatever helps them learn efficiently and enthusiastically. Moreover, teachers who are minimally trained in what these labels mean place much too much power and value in these diagnoses. I remember one educator exclaiming her horror when she discovered that a child had a treatable psychological condition. She really saw this child differently; she pitied him and could only see the disorder—she lost sight of the child himself. It's different with these disorders because they are not well understood and because kids don't grow out of them. If a child was physically ill, no one would say that the child was a *pneumoniac* or a *fluic*, but if a child is autistic, that seems to be all that people see.

When people begin to see the child differently, they then begin to treat the child differently. The child learns to act as if he or she is helpless; indeed, he or she becomes the diagnosis. This is sad. All the potential that was there at birth; all the other parts of the child that are so normal go unrecognized. The child becomes the disorder.

The diagnosis can be used as a crutch, too, as an excuse to not be able to do more. Diagnosis does not belong in the schools. Leave it to the medical profession, the psychiatrists, and the psychologists who have training to keep the diagnosis in perspective, and parents should be advised to always get a second, independent professional opinion. Undoubtedly, teachers need to know how to teach the child, but this can be accomplished without labeling and by opening up services to all children, not just those with labels.

Pessimism is the core result of labeling and diagnosis in our schools. Implied in any diagnosis and label is the unspoken message that there is something wrong with the child, that the child is less capable, that his or her future is potentially changed as a result of this label. Now, any psychologist would say that this is a misunderstanding, and I agree that it is. But, nevertheless, effects of labeling tend to change the expectations of the parents, the teachers, and the children themselves. And the explanation for the child who is not learning is explained by the label rather than by the educational system's failing the child.

Certainly, many educational lawyers like the labels: It makes their jobs black and white. But we are doing a dangerous disservice to these children. Labeling or diagnosing equal an attempt to put the child into a category, and this is not as straightforward as it might appear, because of each individual's uniqueness. Undoubtedly, there is a desire to have a neat, organized cookbook approach to figuring out why a child is not learning, but it is not a clear-cut problem, and it is not always because of weaknesses within the child. Labeling the child keeps us from looking beyond individual weaknesses. It inhibits the discovery of problems within the schools, problems that are interfering with the child's learning. If we start to talk of each child's strengths and needs instead of what is wrong with him or her, we'll be on a much better track.

We seem to be on a craze of more intense labeling, just as we are caught up in the testing craze. Both can be quite harmful to our children; both are hidden dangers within our schools. Recently, we have seen an increase in the number of children being diagnosed with numerous disorders. Some of this increase in diagnosis may reflect an improved ability to diagnose certain disorders. I believe that this is the situation with many of the disorders, such as meningitis, encephalitis, whooping cough, and various flus. But I think much more is involved when we see a sudden jump in the diagnoses of ADHD, autism, Asperger's disorder, and learning disabilities.

Yes, clinicians are becoming more aware, and an accurate diagnosis can be helpful to get the child early intervention, when there is indeed a problem. However, autism and other pervasive development disorders are not well defined, and too many children seem to fall under these umbrella diagnoses. Children who are unique are placed into such categories just because they are misunderstood.

Frequently, the educational interventions would not be different for these children as long as they are learning and receiving assistance to help them acquire social skills and the ability to read social cues. They do not need this label in the schools. Uniqueness should be valued, not treated as a problem.

Let's take a closer look at the characteristics of Asperger's. First of all, it is important to understand that until relatively recently, people who were diagnosed with Asperger's disorder were not classified as having any disorder. They may have been seen as being eccentric, possibly a genius, absented-minded in nature, and somewhat socially and physically awkward. Many such children become extremely interested in a subject—which children don't at some time in their lives? (dinosaurs, horses, computer games)—one that may lead to the individual's becoming extremely successful in a related career later in life.

The most commonly used diagnostic nosologies are the *Diagnostic and Statistical Manual of Mental Disorders* (American Psychiatric Association, 2000) and the *ICD-10: International Classification of Behavioral and Mental Disorders* (World Health Organization, 1992). Both are medical texts. To summarize the perspective of these texts, both view Asperger's disorder as a form of autism, although these individuals diagnosed as such usually function at a higher level. It is a condition that affects the way that a person communicates and relates to others. A number of traits of autism are common to Asperger's disorder, including difficulty in social relationships, difficulty in communicating, and limitations in imagination and creative play. There are many diagnosticians who try to break this category down even further, into subgroups such as high-functioning Asperger's, nonverbal learning disorder, and so on . . . just more and more labels. What it comes down to is that we all could have some sort of label, but what good would it do us? Indeed, it could do us much more harm than good.

There are many well-known people who are alleged to have Asperger's, although formal diagnoses have not been made. I report them here only so that you might begin to question the need for labels and what might have happened had schools labeled and tried to teach these children to learn in more traditional ways. Those diagnosed include Mozart, Albert Einstein, Carl Jung, and Sir Isaac Newton. There are also current-day inventors, businesspeople, musicians, politicians, and leaders from all walks of life who may fit the diagnostic criteria for Asperger's (AspergerResources.com, n.d.).

Now if these individuals have had Asperger's, it was a gift, not a shortcoming. Why on Earth are we bothering to label them? Really, what we should be doing is celebrating their uniqueness, their special qualities, and their fabulous contributions to society and trying to learn from their unique ways of seeing and understanding the world. These are not disordered individuals. To try to "fix" these people is to shortchange their potential. We might be missing out on numerous discoveries and inventions, as well as the gift of diversity. We do not want to limit people or inhibit their growth with a harmful label. Instead, we want to learn to teach each person so that he or she can learn optimally. At the same time, we might just learn something ourselves.

> If a child can't learn the way we teach, maybe we should learn to teach the way they learn.
>
> —Ignacio Estrada

CHAPTER 6

Hidden Dangers: Gender Problems in Our Schools

We are losing young boys to a sense of failure that comes from schooling poorly adapted to their needs. We are losing adolescent males to the depression that comes from feeling neither needed nor respected.

—The Boys Project (n.d., para. 3)

Looking back at our not too distant past, I find it amazing that a common perception was that girls were incapable of learning math or science at an advanced level. Girls were expected to learn the basics that they would need to balance a checkbook, make change at the grocery store, and understand fundamental measurements so that they could handle cookbook recipes. Well, we've come a long way since those days. However, in many ways, we are doing the same thing to our boys today.

Let's take a closer look at Kevin, the adolescent whom we met in Chapter 5. As you remember, Kevin is a 12-year-old of at least high-average intellectual ability, yet his grades do not reflect his academic gifts. He reports that he wants to do well in school, but he does not complete assignments, study for exams, and ask for help when he needs it. We know that he does not have attention deficit hyperactivity disorder (ADHD), and he is not learning disabled. So what is the problem with Kevin?

Could Kevin be one of those fairly typical adolescent males who do not know how to respond in a setting that unintentionally reinforces the positive academic behavior of females? It seems that the male academic needs are not well understood and are often overlooked in our schools. In the case of Kevin, I believe that the issues are far more complex and run deep into the crux of our educational system and our society. Taking a closer look at overall current statistics and trends in our schools can alert us to some of the problems. It seems that girls currently make up 57% of college undergraduates in the United States and that females obtain 58% of all master's degrees awarded in the United States. Furthermore, girls are far outperforming boys in the K–12 academic system. Of those children coded with special needs, 70% are boys, and beginning at the kindergarten level, boys are expected to achieve a standard that favors girls. Girls used to perform less well than boys on standardized tests until the curriculum was changed to meet the needs of girls (Conlin, 2003). Currently, boys are at a disadvantage, with a curriculum that caters to girls and with standardized tests that are developed around the curriculum and so are strongly language oriented (girls tend to excel at earlier ages with language-based approaches).

Clearly, we can see that there are gender issues that need to be addressed. The causes of these gender discrepancies are multifaceted and involve society's perceptions of boys, educational expectations, new state and federal testing policies, school climate, psychological and emotional differences, and brain-based and biological differences. Let's take a closer look at each one of these areas.

Society's perceptions and resulting impact on the gender gap involve confining stereotypes that are a strong part of our cultural and social norms. For example, girls have an unwritten code that demands that they be thin, pretty caregivers, whereas boys are encouraged to be strong, brave, silent, and macho. Pollack (1998) talks about the "boy code," which he describes as an established structure of beliefs regarding how real boys are expected to behave. Unfortunately, these anticipated behaviors clash with expectations in the classroom. These unwritten rules expect boys to act strong and hide their emotions; it's not acceptable for boys to appear vulnerable in any way. As a result, boys are less likely to speak up in the classroom when having difficulty or feeling frustrated; instead, they are more likely to act out or to keep quiet. So, is it possible that Kevin does not ask for help, because he might look less masculine? The answer is a resounding *yes*. Furthermore, this unwritten set of laws is, regrettably, unintentionally and unconsciously reinforced by parents, teachers, coaches, peers, and the media. One can easily see that these societal ideals are disruptive to the lives of both boys and girls. However, it is the male code that appears to have the most negative impact on boys' academic performance.

Problems experienced by males are deeply ingrained within our society's belief system. To get a clear picture of just how profound these beliefs are, all you need do is take a trip to the toy store. Walk down the aisles of the store, and you will immediately be able to tell which aisles are for boys and which are for girls. Most of the toys that are marketed for boys are those with a dark and violent side. These toys reflect and add force to the boy code and sadly reinforce our society's problem of increased violence. Might this play into much of the school violence that we are seeing? I think the answer is very likely *yes*.

The boy code is also implied in many of the common statements that we have all heard or maybe even said, without really understanding the impact that it might have on our male children—for example, "Don't throw like a girl," "Don't walk like a girl," "Be strong, don't cry," and "Don't be a sissy." All are clearly meant to make our boys act in a certain manner. Unfortunately, they trap our boys in a web from which it is difficult for them to escape and so undermines their self-concept.

Furthermore, family interactions have a strong influence on male children. As boys mature, the closeness between family members—particularly, that between mothers and sons—is seen as forbidden. This physical separation starts early for boys and is forced at a time when the child needs emotional and physical closeness, particularly from his parents. A good example is seen when boys first venture into the world to attend preschool. They are expected to leave without a fuss and be brave little men, whereas girls are allowed much more freedom to express their fears and feelings. When the boys hit adolescence, they again are faced with yet another unspoken, strained separation that increases the distance from family members at a crucial time in their lives, when they need guidance, support, and healthy affection from their parents. Pollack (1998) believes that these early separations are a source of depression in many young males. Depression definitely influences academic performance.

Emotionally, boys are at risk in the schools because of these unspoken societal beliefs but also because of educational expectations, policies, and, in many cases, detrimental school climates. Boys are really caught in a catch-22. Case in point, we are less tolerant of boys and expect them to act like little men, to be strong and macho. However, we also expect boys to act the same as girls when it comes to academics: to sit still, color inside the lines, have neat handwriting, work cooperatively, be neat and organized, learn in the same sequence and manner as girls (verbal approach rather than experiential), and demonstrate learning through a standardized testing format that favors girls. Without a doubt, the emotional climate in many schools and classrooms favors girls over boys (Connell & Gunzelmann, 2004; see also Kindlon & Thompson, 2000; Newberger, 1999).

What's more, schools are hurrying children to grow up rapidly and to learn concepts at younger and younger ages. There is a strong downward spiraling of the curriculum and a focus on accountability that has contributed to our current testing obsession. Elkind (2001) believes that our current testing craze is in part due to the dynamics of our hurrying schools. Indeed, boys may be at a unique disadvantage with standardized testing. Although some boys are able to excel in this manner, this approach is far more beneficial to most girls.

A one-size-fits-all approach to testing is not meeting the needs of all of our children. This movement results in no greater knowledge and puts additional stress on our children. Additionally, introducing concepts in earlier grades may put boys at greater risk for failure. Many boys are just not ready to learn many of these concepts, because many of the necessary skills develop later in boys than in girls.

Although boys may be ready to handle certain concepts earlier, these are not usually a part of their early academic curriculum. Actually, the hurrying of the academic curriculum may put both boys and girls in danger of academic problems when content is introduced before a solid foundation is established and before children are cognitively able to comprehend the concepts involved.

All the issues of gender differences can be addressed if we keep in mind the work of Brazelton and Greenspan (2000), who believe that for children to learn and thrive, we must meet their individual needs. Most schools give only lip service to addressing the needs of all children. In fact, individual educational plans are used only for children who are coded with disabilities. Shouldn't the needs of all children be met? Levine (2002) reminds us that "different profiles are destined to make the grade at different times of life depending on when the conditions are right" (p. 37). It appears that we are not yet fully addressing the needs of all individuals and that our boys are definitely paying a high price.

Each and every one of these concerns leads to many boys being misunderstood and even misdiagnosed with ADHD, learning disabilities, oppositional defiant disorder, and conduct disorder when in fact some are just frustrated, poorly taught children. We know from years of research that many more boys are diagnosed with these disorders than girls.

The psychological harm that results from being misunderstood may be significant for boys and include lowered self-esteem, depression, anxiety, and motivational problems. An alarming trend that we are seeing in our country is that younger children are being diagnosed with depression more frequently. Yet, we need to be aware that when boys become depressed, their symptoms may be ignored and misinterpreted because such boys tend to be externalizers. They are seen as being antagonistic, aggressive, antisocial, self-indulgent, and deceitful (Wenar & Kerig, 2000).

Therefore, boys may be misunderstood and thus labeled with oppositional defiant disorder or conduct disorder. They may also have a decreased attention span and an increased activity level as a result of depression rather than ADHD. Depression in children — specifically, in male children — does not always look like adult depression. Adults often become lethargic and withdrawn. Children, particularly boys, often act out and may be misdiagnosed. Boys' symptoms of psychological distress may present differently as well with learning disabilities and with ADHD. There is a wealth of research documenting the large discrepancy in the male–female ratio concerning ADHD diagnoses (cited in Biederman et al., 2002). And there is comorbidity of ADHD with conduct, depressive, anxiety, and learning disorders, as well as substance abuse and other disorders (Biederman, Newcorn, & Sprich, 1991). Such constant misunderstanding and awkwardness of fit with one's academic endeavors may lead to a self-defeating downward spiral of issues, resulting in lowered academic performance.

There are also biologically based differences in boys' and girls' brains. Human brains consist of two hemispheres that are intricately connected; however, they process information differently (Baron-Cohen, 2003; Springer & Deutsch, 1998). The left hemisphere processes information analytically and sequentially, which allows this hemisphere to focus on details. The left hemisphere has primary responsibility for processing auditory and verbal information. The left brain specializes in comprehending words and is actively involved in listening, speaking, and writing. In contrast, the processing style of the right hemisphere is intuitive and holistic; it sees the whole picture. The right hemisphere is usually where visual–spatial and visual–motor information is processed. As such, our right brain specializes in activities such as sports, architecture, sculpture, painting, and carpentry (Connell, 2002).

So, when boys and girls begin kindergarten and first grade at the same ages, they have different developmental strengths and weaknesses. Girls' left hemispheres are more developed than those of boys (Gurian, 2001). In essence, brain biology permits girls to read and write using the traditional approaches at a younger age. In contrast, according to Gurian, boys' right hemispheres are more developed, allowing them to more easily learn using nontraditional approaches involving movement and visual–spatial skills. These brain-based differences have been documented in the research using norm-referenced intelligence and achievement measures. Vogel (1990) writes,

> In general for the normally achieving population, a substantial body of research confirms the higher verbal ability of females including global verbal abilities as measured by the WISC Verbal subtests, grammar, word fluency, and spelling and higher visual-spatial and mathematical abilities of males. (p. 50)

Conventionally, teachers have encouraged boys to learn to read and write in a traditional manner, understanding that, developmentally, boys would catch up around the fourth grade. Our country's current focus on high-stakes state and federal tests generally works in favor of the brain strengths of girls and against those of boys, especially at the lower grade levels. Achievement data from No Child Left Behind show that in all 50 states, boys are behind girls in reading and math. However, these test scores do not give an accurate picture of boys' abilities. For instance, boys can learn their letters by first making the letters out of clay; they can act out the punctuation marks; and they can read by incorporating phonics using technology (Connell & Gunzelmann, 2004).

Although boys used to catch up with the girls around fourth grade, this is no longer the case. Today, with the pressure of the state and federal tests experienced by teachers and students alike, boys are feeling pressure and stress that is harmful to them. Instead of catching up, they are giving up. School is often seen by boys as "a girl thing" (Connell & Gunzelmann, 2004).

So, what can we do to improve this dreadful academic situation for boys? Clearly, there are psychological and biological differences between boys and girls that result in differences in the way that society perceives boys, how parents and the schools interact with male students, and what the resulting emotional responses of boys are. For the past 30 years, our girls have been supported by the influential women's movement. In 1972, Congress passed Title IX, which provides gender equity in schools across America. Today, there is increased awareness by professors, teachers, and parents throughout the country who encourage girls to take advanced courses, participate in sports, and do their best work. Clearly, we need to continue to support our girls; however, at the same time, we must also begin to focus on ways to help our boys. It's time to address the individual needs of all children.

There are numerous things that we can do to help all children succeed academically. First and foremost, we can create positive and supportive home and school environments for all children by challenging the boy code and the unwritten girl code. We all need to confront our beliefs about how boys and girls should look and behave. Boys can be genuine boys and not be caught in a catch-22 if we encourage them to express their feelings and be true to themselves. They should not be forced into false roles to fit in. Girls should be encouraged to accept themselves for who they are—they do not need to fit some ideal Barbie Doll image and live up to a superwoman's standard. They can also be quite feminine and successful. Strong, healthy male and female role models are needed in our schools, models who are not buying into these unhealthy codes (Gunzelmann & Connell, 2006).

We can also change curriculum and the teaching approaches. Why not introduce concepts to boys on their timetable; allowing for individual and gender differences is essential. Many boys are not ready to sit still and color between the lines at young ages. They should not be made to feel inferior by receiving lower grades, being reprimanded, and being medicated because they develop at different rates than girls. We don't need to change the boys, but we definitely need to change the methods, including the assessment approaches (Connell & Gunzelmann, 2004; Gunzelmann & Connell, 2006).

In closing, as counselors, teachers, and parents, we have our work cut out for us—we must keep the girls soaring while opening the cage and letting the boys fly, too. The key is to understand that the boys' flight patterns are different from the girls': We must acknowledge and encourage both.

> Many boys think that their grade schools are boy-unfriendly. I well remember my son bursting into the kitchen one day after school, yelling "They want us to be girls, Mom, they want us to be girls!"
>
> —P. Dalton ("When Did We Lose Sight of Boys?" *Washington Post*, May 9, 1999; as cited in IllinoisLoop.org., 2006a, para. 3)

CHAPTER 7

Hidden Dangers: Paradoxical Safety Problems in Our Schools

Listen to your children. They will tell you, perhaps not directly but by their behavior, whether they feel safe at school.

—Merrow (2001, p. 104)

Safety in the schools involves much more than metal detectors and disaster plans. Although such catastrophe planning is necessary, we are overlooking some less obvious issues that put our children's everyday safety and education at risk. It appears that some of our current practices designed to ensure student safety are actually increasing safety concerns. As we learned in Chapter 2 from Brazelton and Greenspan (2000), all children require physical protection, safety, and regulation in order to grow, learn, and flourish. The obvious safety issues are clear-cut and usually well addressed in our schools. However, there are less obvious, paradoxical hidden dangers in our schools that influence the social, cognitive, and emotional well-being of our students.

These hidden dangers are not always apparent, and they may be taken for granted as being helpful and therefore not problematic. However, I believe that these risks are contributing to a crisis that includes school violence, behavioral and emotional problems, students' being unable to attain basic skills, and students' feeling unsafe.

PARADOXICAL REACTIONS TO SAFETY POLICIES

Since the Columbine shootings and September 11, we have seen a dramatic increase in cases of posttraumatic stress disorder and other anxiety disorders, as well as an increase in cases of depression. Given that the issues in our schools reflect the larger issues seen in our society, it is not surprising that there is an increase in anxiety disorders and depression among our school-age children. I suspect that this increase is in part due to the overreaction of many adults in an attempt to protect our children that may unintentionally be increasing our children's stress levels and, paradoxically, making our schools less safe than before. School lockdowns, armed police in the schools, metal detectors, crisis response teams, surveillance cameras, and other high-tech law enforcement personnel procedures and equipment are now quite common in our school buildings. In fact, schools are becoming increasingly similar to jails and juvenile detention centers—certainly not a climate conducive to enhanced academic learning.

Clearly, we all have much to learn from the work of our law enforcement agencies, and their services are vital to our society. One very enlightening document regarding school violence was published as a joint endeavor by the U.S. Secret Service and the Department of Education (2002) titled *The Final Report and Findings of the Safe School Initiative: Implications for the Prevention of School Attacks in the United States*. Undoubtedly, this document is a reflection of our society over the past many years, and there is a considerable amount of well-conducted research and information generated from this effort. Nonetheless, when one reads it and looks at how this information has been interpreted and applied in our schools, it becomes obvious that we really need to make some adjustments. I am in no way criticizing this important document; I am merely trying to look at what else might be needed and assess the fallout from faulty attempts to make our schools safer places.

I was initially surprised to see the Secret Service working with the Department of Education, but the benefit of these agencies combining their expertise soon became apparent. However, what also became clear as I read the report was the mind-set in the interpretation of data obtained from previous school violence incidents: It was interpreted primarily from a martial and law enforcement perspective. What was glaringly left out of this report was the vast amount of accumulated knowledge from educators, psychologists, sociologists, pediatricians, and other professionals with child development expertise. There needs to be much more collaboration in conducting the research, interpreting the results, and, most important, implementing the findings.

We are truly out of balance in our schools when we do not approach educating our children with an evenhanded perspective gleaned from all experts in related fields. Instead, the balance has shifted toward an adult reactionary need to anticipate, plan, and control every conceivable catastrophe, which inadvertently makes all of us more wary, uneasy, and anxious—yet, really no safer. It is irrational to believe that we can control for every possibility that may happen; nor should we be worrying our children about every possible tragedy that could intrude on their lives. It can be equated with having drills in the schools for how one should react if a meteor hit the building; the likelihood of this occurrence is slight. In the event that it did happen, then the adults in charge would call in whatever emergency services were needed. Certainly, our military, police, firefighters, and emergency medical teams need to have specific training to deal with crises, and the general public should be advised of planned procedures, but our children should not have to worry and be overwhelmed by the changing world in which we are living.

Regrettably, children are learning that the world is not safe, but they are also learning that their schools are not safe places either. All that children need to do to confirm these ideas is to look around on any given day to observe metal detectors, armed police, lockdown drills, and various other disaster-planning maneuvers being played out in their classrooms. These so-called safety measures are sometimes acted out in full riot gear, requiring the children to put cardboard over the windows and remain silent and hide under their desks. Teachers are required to do the same. If a child is left out in the hallway or has been to the bathroom, he or she no longer has access to the hypothetical safety zone within the classroom.

The professionals in charge here really need to stop and ask the question "What are we thinking here?" To a young child these drills are nothing short of terrifying, with police charging around with guns and with their parents not being allowed into the buildings. Young children are being emotionally harmed by these drills, which are occurring in most schools across the country. What we are doing is teaching our children to be fearful, that their neighborhood is a dangerous place to be. This is not to say that the world isn't a dangerous place today; certainly, it is. But we can help our children to know basic safety behaviors without causing permanent harm to their fundamental sense of trust. Have we all forgotten the well-known psychosocial theory of Erik Erikson? The first and critical stage is for children to be able to develop a basic sense of trust before they are able to move on to higher stages. Most parents do an exemplary job helping their infants learn to trust during their early years. This critical foundation is essential to negotiating higher stages, and current practices are eroding this essential base. Psychologists, educators, and other child development specialists are also aware of Abraham Maslow's work on human motivation and the implications on learning. Maslow's theory clearly depicts the indispensable need of safety, near the base of the hierarchy, which is needed well before one can feel a sense of belonging and self-esteem and then begin the learning tasks at hand (for a summary of Maslow's and Erickson's theories, see Schultz & Schultz, 2001).

We also must consider the cognitive developmental levels of the children. Jean Piaget's widely researched and replicated studies clearly show that children do not think in the same manner as most adults. Children, particularly preteens, are not able to think in "what if" terms. They may see in these practice drills that the real event is likely to happen. Thus, the younger the child, the more vulnerable he or she is to this harmful misunderstanding, and the less able he or she is to comprehend that there isn't a terrorist standing right around the corner or lurking in the next classroom.

Indeed, we will see more issues of anxiety, hopelessness, and difficulties learning. Even more concerning are those malleable young minds that get caught up in the excitement and the intensity of the drama and begin to identify with the need to fight violence with violence. Albert Bandura's social learning theory (1977) clearly demonstrates how children copy their models. Children may not be able to learn their academic subjects under such highly stressful conditions, but you can be sure that they will be learning from the models of force parading around the schools.

Are we drawing so much attention to these issues through the news, media, and by our overresponses that schools may be inadvertently encouraging copycat behavior and reinforcing school violence? This is a dangerous practice, indeed. (For more information about Bandura's theory, see Schultz & Schultz, 2001.)

We are truly out of balance in our schools when we take into account their martial mentality. It may make many adults feel more in control to be doing something in the name of safety, but it really is an illusion. There is a hidden curriculum demanding obedience and conformity in many of our schools (Mosca & Hollister, 2004; Saltman & Gabbard, 2003). Furthermore, young people are quickly realizing that schools have more in common with military boot camps and prisons than they do with other institutions in American society (Giroux, 2003).

Let's consider, for example, the zero-tolerance policies that many schools now have in place. A zero-tolerance policy has no openmindedness for any wrongdoing, no matter how inconsequential and understandable a situation may be. We need to question our need for such extreme policies. On first hearing of such policies, parents may believe that zero tolerance as a concept will help to make a school a safer place to be. But like so many other plans in life, what might look good on paper plays out quite differently in real life. We must ask ourselves why we think such drastic measures are a current need.

Are most of our children so out of control that they don't know right from wrong? Reverend Jesse Jackson believes, "Fear of our children is at the heart of zero tolerance policies in our schools" (quoted in Mosca & Hollister, 2004, vii; see also Ayers, Dohrn, & Ayers, 2001). I think he may be right. Zero tolerance is reinforcing the belief that children cannot be trusted.

Many schools have adopted zero-tolerance policies, particularly concerning weapons, drugs, and alcohol. At first glance, these policies may appear to make sense and to protect our children, but in actuality, they can be quite detrimental and at times may even increase the risk to children. The American Psychological Association's Zero Tolerance Task Force reviewed research on the effects of zero-tolerance policies over a 10-year period and determined "that such policies not only fail to make schools safe or more effective in handling student behavior, they actually increase the instances of problem behavior and dropout rates" (quoted in Farberman, 2006, p. 27). There are numerous extreme zero-tolerance cases that can be cited to depict the problems inherent in these policies. Consider, for example, the case of an adolescent male who used mouthwash on school premises. Because the mouthwash contained alcohol, he was harshly punished, with the police being called in. This young man did not drink the mouthwash; he merely used it to freshen his breath, which is an age-appropriate behavior for self-conscious adolescents (ZTNightmares.com, 2003).

There are also numerous well-documented cases of harsh and unreasonable consequences resulting from zero-tolerance policies. Included in these cases are incidents involving the writing of a scary Halloween story as a class assignment, stealing $2 from another student, and the vague threat by a 12-year-old in a school lunch line that he was "going to get" students if they ate all the potatoes. Unbelievably, this child spent 2 weeks in jail! (American Bar Association, 2000; for cases and alarming statistics, see Black, 2004; Koch, 2000). In so many cases, it appears the zero-tolerance policies trump reason. In the cases reported here, the authorities were called in, and no one listened to the individual circumstances involved. In numerous cases, responsible young people have faced legal procedures and potential youth imprisonment, to the horror of their parents and friends. These unfortunate situations have resulted in needless legal cases, undue hardship for parents, and, regrettably, an extreme distrust toward the schools and various authority figures.

Another important finding is that zero-tolerance policies unfairly target minority and disadvantaged youth. One of the most infamous cases occurred in Decatur, Illinois, where seven students were expelled for a 2-year period after a brawl at a high school football game. Jesse Jackson believed that the harsh disciplinary action was racially biased, and he was instrumental in having the ruling reduced (PBS.org, 2007). It appears that there are alarming statistics depicting that zero-tolerance policies appear to unfairly discriminate, as reported by the American Educational Research Association and a 2001 report from Harvard University's Civil Rights Project (cited in Black, 2004). According to a report from the American Psychological Association Zero Tolerance Task Force (2006), zero-tolerance policies in schools can actually increase school violence and behavior problems. "The task force reviewed ten years of research on the effects of zero tolerance policies in middle and secondary schools and concluded that such policies not only fail to make schools safe or more effective in handling student behavior, they actually increase the instances of problem behavior and drop out rates" (Farberman, 2006, p. 27).

It appears that students who are learning disabled are also over-represented as offenders of zero-tolerance policies, as are students from lower socioeconomic levels (Harvard University, Civil Rights Project, 2003). Clearly, zero-tolerance policies are not conducive to safe school environments. Instead, zero-tolerance policies may be establishing dangerous school climates.

So just what are our children learning from such extreme measures? They are learning not to tell people in authority when they suspect that someone might have a dangerous weapon or may be threatening another. To the children, particularly to adolescents, the adults do not listen and overreact to the slightest situations; thus, children do not want to get their friends in trouble over a potentially small incident. They also do not want to be put in the position of being a "nark" or a tattletale, a compromising social situation for any child. Consequently, during a genuinely serious threat, students may not speak up.

Furthermore, harassment, threats, and intimidation of students routinely take place when zero-tolerance policies are in effect. This only increases our teens' distrust and alienation from adults, and it increases their own anxieties about being in a school climate that clearly does not trust or respect the students. This brat-camp mentality establishes schools that are not places of learning but are places where control is paramount and differences are seen as threats. These are schools that break the spirit of our youth. Children become hopeless, anxious, depressed, and pessimistic—alienated from their true selves. These are toxic climates, indeed.

The zero-tolerance policies go against all that we know that we should do in the schools. As adults, we need to take each case on an individualized basis, listen to the child, and understand the whole situation. Even the American Bar Association (2000) voted against mandatory zero-tolerance policies in the schools; still, more and more schools are adopting these regulations.

> Fear and reactionary politics rather than sound reasoning, have driven the zero tolerance movement and led, in fact, to schools that are less safe.
>
> —Mosca and Hollister (2004, p. 4)

SOCIAL HARMS: BULLIES AND CLIQUES

There are other red-flag issues pertaining to our children's safety that we must become more aware of. One of the biggest problems in our schools involves bullying. School administrators are well aware that bullying occurs, and they spend a great deal of time and energy developing antibullying policies. So often, antibullying programs and policies look good on paper but are ineffective and even ignored by students and school personnel.

Bullying is a widespread phenomenon that involves tormenting victims through various means, including all types of harassment, assault, and attempts to manipulate or coerce victims. It can take several destructive forms, including verbal, physical, sexual, racial, and emotional. One of the more recent developments involves cyber bullying, which occurs through e-mail, instant messaging, cell phones, text messaging, and other technological approaches. Cyber bullying can be severely harmful, reaching the victim in the shelter of his or her home, and it instantaneously spreads the vicious messages to untold numbers across the Internet.

Children who are bullied suffer from anxiety, depression, and lowered self-esteem. Bullying interferes with learning as well. Over time, children who are bullied may repeatedly retreat and feel hopeless; they may become angry and act out. Oftentimes, children who are the bullies engage in antisocial acts. Emotional bullying can be more subtle but no less damaging. School lunchrooms are notorious for this type of bullying, where students are shunned and not allowed to sit at certain tables. This type of abuse occurs frequently because of cliques, which are destructive and should not be confused with groups of friends. It's healthy to have a strong peer group with similar interests, but cliques involve a strict code of membership and behavior in order to belong. The purpose of a clique is for status and popularity where a friendship involves shared values and beliefs (Kids Health, 2005). Girls tend to engage in verbal, emotional, and cyber bullying, whereas boys get involved with the physical types of abuse. Both genders can be quite cruel, particularly in middle school grades when they may not realize the extent of harm and pain that they are causing their classmates. Racial slurs and sexual innuendo are particularly damaging to the developing sense of self.

Another serious concern is that school personnel at times engage in bullying and harassing the students, too. "Children are quietly tormented in ways that adults in charge appear to either willfully ignore or silently approve" (Meier, 2004, p. 58). On numerous occasions, I have heard of teachers using intimidation tactics to get students to behave in a desired manner. Calling a student a name, even when it is meant in jest, is more harmful when coming from an adult in authority. Names such as *space cadet*, *hyper*, and *lazy* are damaging labels that can have long-term implications. Names such as *idiot*, *jerk*, and *stupid* have no business being on the lips of teachers either but have been reported by teacher-bullied students on numerous occasions. I realize that children—particularly, adolescents—can push adults to say things that they do not mean. However, if this happens, the adults must be aware of the damaging effects of their statements and thus make amends.

School personnel at times ignore or gloss over bullying when they see it in the schools. For example, one student described a scene in a seventh-grade classroom that occurred when a couple from the popular clique made derogatory remarks to a girl about her appearance and her clumsy behavior. The teacher's response was to quietly laugh, which encourages this type of bullying to continue. This young girl has reportedly been bullied since kindergarten. Why would a teacher do such a thing? Well, I'm not sure that the teacher was even aware of his behavior. This was not an intentionally mean adult; I suspect that he unconsciously did not want to confront the girls of the popular clique and lose face in their eyes. You see, he was seen as one of the "cool teachers" (teachers have their cliques, too!).

Then there is the case of Luke, who is an adolescent who complained that school went against his learning and development. Socially, he did not fit in the cool cliques, and at times, he was bullied by some of the other students. Although school personnel tried to help him with "his" problem, in some ways the faculty and staff were a part of the problem. Some believed that he just needed to toughen up, whereas others overprotected him. Both approaches left Luke feeling inadequate and unsafe in his academic environment.

When reviewing statistics on school violence, numerous cases involve severe and prolonged bullying. Our schools are not safe when bullying is occurring. Why is this being allowed to happen in our schools? Bullying is not a normal part of childhood behavior. It is learned behavior and has become deeply ingrained in many school cultures. But what our children need to learn is to respect, understand, and appreciate individual differences and diversity, not to shun or bully classmates for their uniqueness. A quote from J. Noonan (2004) sums up the social ills affecting school safety:

> The development of strong and sustainable relationships will contribute more in the end to a healthy and safe school than metal detectors ever will, and our ability to instruct our students how to develop sustainable relationships of their own is as essential a skill as math and reading. (p. 65)

OUT-OF-CONTROL CLASSROOMS

Although there are problems contributing to safety issues in the schools, there are also times when some children need special placements where they will be accepted while they are working on their behaviors so that they can successfully be included in regular classrooms. In Chapter 3, we were introduced to the case of Sally. Her situation illustrates problems which occur frequently. To refresh your memory, Sally was experiencing symptoms of anxiety and attention problems, not from a deficit of her own, but because of an out-of-control classroom. Out of a class of 28 children, two students had severe behavioral problems and required a lot of extra time from the teacher, who had no education or experience to handle problems of this magnitude.

Teachers cannot handle all the severe issues that are being mainstreamed into their classrooms. Schools have been including children in regular classrooms under the guise that they be allowed to have the same educational experience as other children. I couldn't agree more completely, as long as other children are not put at risk of injury or are continually deprived of instruction time and as long as the mainstreamed child is receiving the best educational interventions and not just passing time, as is so often the case. Schools do this to save money. Having too many children in out-of-district placement costs a lot of money. However, if the child receives the appropriate schooling early (without the need for a label and without the needless and excessive costs of educational lawyers), then all children will benefit, and more serious problems will be prevented. Children who are underserviced in the schools or for whom the school just is not a good fit are oftentimes the ones being bullied and developing secondary problems, sometimes with quite serious ramifications.

CURRICULUM CONCERNS

One other serious hidden safety concern that really needs to be revamped involves relatively common curricular selections. Children are impressionable; we all know this fact. We also know that it is more difficult to keep children interested in the classroom today than it was 30 and 40 years ago. Today's children are used to technology with all its special effects; they can easily become bored with the curriculum. In an attempt to make the classroom an interesting place, many teachers resort to curriculum that is definitely sensation seeking but may be contributing to problems for our children. I'm referring to programs of study that include the darker side of children's literature, where violence and suicide are not uncommon themes; to science lectures that focus more on the "guts and gore" than on understanding the process; and even to history lessons that use Hollywood-version movies about wars, all in an attempt to entertain the children. Unfortunately, they are learning lessons that teachers never meant to teach, and as a result, our children are at more emotional risk. We may be contributing to children's increasing rate of anxiety, depression, and even violence.

The well-documented classic research of Bandura (1965) and numerous other current social–cognitive theorists partially explains my concerns here. Humans and animals are capable of *vicarious learning*, or learning by observing others. The models presented in some children's literature, movies, and so on, are not necessarily the ones that we want our children modeling. Of course, not all children will perform such undesirable behaviors. However, under certain circumstances and with the right consequences, some children will perform them. Even more disturbing is the fact that all children who were exposed to such models have learned the behavior whether they act on it or not. I believe that we have a responsibility to make sure that our children are exposed to healthy models whenever possible and to *take the time* to help children process and fully understand the situations when they inevitably come across harmful models in the news and their everyday lives.

In précis, we must be cognizant of what we teach and how we teach, of our safety policies and procedures, and of assisting our children in overcoming the negative pressures within our culture that encourage cliques and bullying. Furthermore, we must develop safer school climates that foster an appreciation for individual differences and diversity. Then, our schools will be safer places for our children to thrive.

> It may be that only when we create truly more interesting schools will they be safer places. In short, too much of our discussion of safety misses the real target.
>
> —Meier (2004, p. 55)

CHAPTER 8

Hidden Dangers in Our School Buildings

There are numerous hidden dangers in our school buildings that many parents assume are being properly handled, because schools are public buildings and they house our most precious resource: our children. However, this may not be the case. Many of our nation's school facilities are outdated, with problems such as asbestos and a host of environmental contaminants. Even in newer buildings, there are real causes for concern. For example, some new school buildings have been erected on landfills. The land was available and the price was right, but what about the toxic chemicals just below the surface? To think that our children are playing on playgrounds that were once dumps—what are officials thinking here?

Let's take a closer look at some of these very real concerns in our schools today. Our country is growing rapidly. According to information from the U.S. Census Bureau (2000), the U.S. population reached 281,421,906 in 2000 with current estimates (2007) over 299,000,000 (Population Reference Bureau, 1999). Furthermore, the Census Bureau claims that the population is rising rapidly and will continue to do so. With statistics such as these, we undoubtedly have a growth problem and a real predicament with providing safe and first-rate schools for our nation's children.

It is understandable, with the current and projected population growth rates, that the U.S. Environmental Protection Agency (EPA) is looking into the feasibility of allowing more schools to be built on *brownfields*. According to the U.S. EPA (2007b), a brownfield site is "real property, the expansion, redevelopment, or reuse of which may be complicated by the presence or potential presence of a hazardous substance, pollutant, or contaminant" (para. 1).

The Brownfields Revitalization Act became law in 2002. This law provides financial assistance to eligible applicants, and apparently, schools are allowed to use such brownfields to build educational facilities once these sites are cleaned up. The land is available, and the price is considerably lower than purchasing virgin or other prime real estate. Vague terminology is being used, such as *sufficiently decontaminated*, when there are no established levels of safety available based on long-term research. Determining what might be a sufficient level of decontamination is a risky practice given that children are much more susceptible to toxins in the environment than are otherwise healthy adults because children's nervous and endocrine systems are less well developed and much more susceptible to harmful chemical messengers. Basically, the younger the child, the more the susceptibility (Children's Environmental Health Network, 2005). Therefore, without long-term research on the effects of these supposedly cleaned-up sites, I believe that we are playing Russian roulette with the lives of our children. Certainly, these sites do need to be cleaned up, but the use of such reclaimed sites should be for other sustainable purposes than educating our children. Trying to save a buck yet risking the very futures of our children and, ultimately, our nation seems penny-wise and pound-foolish.

AIR QUALITY

Air quality is another major concern in our nation's schools. By reviewing anecdotal information, the news stories, and a variety of other sources, we can easily detect that a range of indoor air problems are occurring and thus result in costly and time-consuming interventions, including school evacuations and emergency repairs. Astoundingly, in 1996, the U.S. Government Accounting Office released data indicating that over half of our schools have problems that affect indoor air quality.

Many of our nation's schools were built in the 1950s and earlier, when building codes and related safety concerns were not as compelling. We now know that there are significant health-related issues related to asbestos, radon, toxic molds, pesticides, numerous cleaning products, and even glues and other toxins used in the building and carpeting of new schools. Nonetheless, there seems to be a disconnect between health and safety issues based on solid research and the repairing of these building violations and the necessary precautions for use of new materials and products.

Many building materials, even those used a decade or two ago, have been banned, including products with asbestos, which is in numerous building materials: floor and ceiling tiles, older siding and roofing products, and walls, as well as heating elements and insulation. Certainly, the mitigation of asbestos from our schools is a costly process but one that needs to be addressed sooner rather than later (see U.S. Environmental Protection Agency, 2007a).

Many schools are still in the process of making such repairs; others have done so but may have had shoddy work done. Additionally, air-quality testing should be done on a routine basis to ensure that levels remain safe. Why has it taken so long to address this issue in our schools when the risk of asbestos exposure has been know for many years now? And why is it that in many instances, the general public was not well aware of such concerns?

We know that there is no established safe level of asbestos, so we need to be vigilant to make sure that our children are exposed to as little as possible. Back in May 2000, headline news focused on the fact that asbestos had been found in children's crayons (Schneider & Smith, 2000). Even the Consumer Product Safety Commission (2000) was caught off guard by these findings. Apparently, the talc used in crayons, to make them less waxy, may have asbestos mixed in as a result of the mining process. This just goes to show that all products used by children should be regularly monitored for quality standards.

Radon is another serious health concern, one not usually addressed in our schools. Radon can have harmful effects in our drinking water and in our air. If the water is from public sources, the radon levels are carefully monitored. If water is obtained from private sources, then the radon levels may or may not be addressed. We know that repeated, prolonged exposure to radon causes lung cancer in smokers and nonsmokers (U.S. Environmental Protection Agency, 2007f). Yet, according to the EPA, radon-related examination of 29 schools across the country resulted in poor ventilation being discovered in most of the schools. Also, nearly one in five schools is estimated to have at least one classroom with radon measures above the EPA's recommended safety levels (U.S. Environmental Protection Agency, 2007f; see also U.S. Environmental Protection Agency, 1994). These are concerning findings, no doubt. But the most disturbing information is that radon testing is not routinely conducted in the schools. It is done on only a voluntary basis. Furthermore, if radon is detected, the school may or may not choose to address the problem. The EPA has no regulatory or enforcement authority regarding general indoor air quality in our nation's schools. This is outrageous. Living in a nation where school buildings are aging and are subjected to the powerful effects of nature—storms, winds, ice, temperature changes—raises the possibilities of cracking, settling, and leaking. Leaks bring water damage, which frequently results in the build-up of toxic molds (see U.S. Environmental Protection Agency, 2007e; Santilli, 2002).

The case of Carol clearly illustrates the serious consequences of molds in school buildings. Carol is an only child of an intact professional family. Carol's parents changed their daughter's school during third grade because of chronic health problems. She was allergic to high levels of mold in her school building and was frequently sick from secondary infections. As a result, she needed to be on allergy medication, which caused her to feel tired and unmotivated. The side effects of the medication and the numerous absences from school interfered with her academic progress. Carol's parents consulted her medical doctors and, as a result, requested that the school building be tested for molds not routinely considered during air quality assessment. The results came back positive for elevated levels of mold contamination. School administrators wanted to code (label) the child with the problem when in reality it was the building that was unhealthy and unsafe for all of its inhabitants.

Unfortunately, Carol developed multiple antibiotic allergies complicated by frequent and chronic usage of them due to infections that would not clear while she remained in the polluted school environment. We know that the need for extensive use of antibiotics is a risk to all our citizens because bacteria build resistance to antibiotics at an alarming rate and drugs become ineffective, thereby allowing for the development of super bugs, which do not respond to typical antibiotic treatment. Medical researchers are discovering that

> in the United States and globally, many other infectious germs, including those that cause pneumonia, ear infections, acne, gonorrhea, urinary tract infections, meningitis, and tuberculosis, can now outwit some of the most commonly used antibiotics and their synthetic counterparts, antimicrobials. According to the Mayo Clinic in Rochester, Minn., drug resistance may have contributed to the 58 percent rise in infectious disease deaths among Americans between 1980 and 1992. (Nordenberg, 1998, para. 3)

Furthermore, Dr. David Bell of the Centers for Disease Control and Prevention (CDC) states that "virtually all important human pathogens treatable with antibiotics have developed some resistance" (quoted in Nordenberg, 1998, para. 5). As such, the CDC believes this resistance to be one the world's most pressing public health problems.

Carol was forced to change schools because she was always sick with secondary infections owing to the severity of the pollution and to the lack of responsiveness to the contamination by school personnel. Once her school environment changed, Carol no longer suffered from chronic secondary sinus infections. For her, most common colds ran a more typical course; she never needed antibiotic interventions; and she found it much easier to focus on her academic studies. Her case represents only one example of the serious health and safety issues that clearly affect the long-term well-being and academic success of all of our children.

Asthma and allergies have been increasing at alarming rates over the past many years. In 2003, the CDC estimated that 19.8 million Americans were diagnosed with asthma, indicating a serious health problem impacting the United States (Center for Disease Control, 2005). Furthermore, the National Heart, Lung, and Blood Institute reported asthma symptoms doubling during the previous 15 years (cited in National Institutes of Health, 2001), and in the United States alone, the rates of mortality from asthma, hospitalizations, and emergency room visits have been increasing, especially among children and African American populations. We can no longer afford to ignore these alarming statistics and evidence that indoor pollutants trigger asthma and related problems in our children and school personnel (see National Institute of Environmental Health Services, 2006).

OTHER SCHOOL ENVIRONMENTAL CONCERNS

The well-being of a school building is overlooked as a safety issue, but it is a real concern that affects the learning and health of all of our children. Carol's issues were specific and could clearly be documented. But we need to question the health and safety of our schools in others areas as well—areas that may not be as easy to measure except with longitudinal studies.

The manner in which our school buildings are renovated, remodeled, and newly built needs to be carefully scrutinized for the materials being used. For instance, many schools use carpeting to cover floor tiles containing asbestos. First of all, this is not an adequate intervention for containing the potentially friable asbestos particles, particularly when carpeting needs to be replaced and is thus torn up, thereby disturbing the tiles underneath.

Even in new school buildings where carpeting is used to cut down on noise levels, a host of environmental concerns arise. When the synthetic carpeting is new, residual chemicals leach into the environment from the adhesives used and from the synthetic materials in the carpets themselves. Such chemical contaminants can cause a variety of allergies and chemical sensitivities, thus affecting health, behavior, and learning.

Carpets also hold dust mites, pet dander, and other common allergens, increasing the potential for students' and teachers' allergic and asthmatic reactions. When children spill their milk and other drinks (as all children do) and when buildings leak (as all buildings do), carpeting becomes a breeding ground for mold with all its inherent problems discussed earlier.

This brings us to the toxic chemicals used to clean school buildings, even those used to inhibit the growth of molds. Many chemical cleaners are considered pesticides, with serious potential health risks. Most public schools today have lists of cleaning products that are acceptable when used under specific guidelines. But we should clearly understand that these chemicals are highly noxious and, to many people, actually disrupt their ability to function in these environments. We can all probably remember returning after a vacation to a school with cleaned and polished floors. Even these polishes contain potentially harmful ingredients that cause many people to feel nauseated and to have headaches as a result. These individuals may be more sensitive, but these chemicals are not good for anyone.

We should also be aware that regular pesticide application is routine for many of our schools to prevent insects, rodents, and other undesirable creatures from taking over the buildings. With the use of many of these chemicals, we are contaminating the very environment that we are trying to protect. The U.S. Environmental Protection Agency (1992) reports that all pesticides are poisonous to some extent. Even the fertilizers and weed killers used to beautify the school grounds are putting our children at risk. Additionally, we must remember that children are more sensitive than adults to harmful chemicals because of their size, development, and the differences in how they interact with the environment. Children are much more likely to play on the lawns, playgrounds, and sports fields and to sit on the floor inside and outside their school buildings. At times, some of these chemicals are accidentally ingested through unwashed hands. Pesticides are frequently used in the schools in the cafeterias, kitchens, classrooms, offices, locker rooms, bathrooms, storage rooms, basements, and even in day care rooms. Parents and students are often not aware when these applications occur (see also U.S. Environmental Protection Agency, 2002).

Pesticides have a long list of related exposure problems, including acute and long-term risks of headache, nausea, dizziness, abdominal cramps, vision problems, weight loss, toxic psychosis, convulsions, skin irritations, vomiting, sensory and behavioral problems, sweating, coughing spasms, reproductive effects, anorexia, ulcers of the mouth and pharynx, and cancer. Clearly, all systems in the human body may be affected (U.S. Environmental Protection Agency, 1989).

According to the Natural Resources Defense Council (2000), peeling or chipping paint is considered an immediate threat. Small children are more susceptible to toxins, and eating as little as one paint chip can be harmful. If such paint is left intact, it deteriorates over time and may release toxic lead dust. However, the removal of lead paint can potentially release even higher levels of lead dust inside a school. Clearly, experienced contractors must be consulted when addressing such hazards. Lead paint in children causes headaches; stomach pain; anemia; damage to the nervous system, kidneys, and/or hearing; speech and language problems; decreased bone and muscle growth; delayed development; and with notably high levels, seizures and unconsciousness (Kids Health, 2006).

Conclusive evidence is not yet available regarding some of the newer products and technology used in our schools. Even the use of certain lighting in the schools needs to be questioned. Fluorescent and high-density discharge lamps damage our environment if disposed of improperly, owing to the mercury content in them. The use of technology may increase our exposure to potentially harmful environmental factors as well. Testing so far is not definitive in these areas, but at least research studies are occurring. Looking back over these chapters, I find it a wonder that we are still able to get up in the morning and get ourselves out the door. But we cannot be consumed with fear, nor should we just dismiss these issues by saying such trivializing statements as "Well, this is just the world we live in."

No, it doesn't have to be this dangerous, and we need to pay attention to our environments when we are seeing such serious increases in learning and behavioral problems, attention deficit disorders, autism spectrum disorders, anxiety issues, depression, suicide, increased violence, allergies, asthma, childhood obesity and eating disorders, let alone increases in cancer and other serious health problems. The hidden dangers in our schools are putting our nation at risk.

> All students have the right to expect a safe and healthy environment. . . . The health of our children demands no less.
>
> —Keith Geiger (National Education Association president, quoted in U.S. Environmental Protection Agency, 2007f, para. 8)

CHAPTER 9

Safe and Healthy School Climates

Now that we have a better understanding of the hidden dangers within our schools, it's time to look at the other side of the coin, to identify what makes a school a safe place for our children—a place where learning is deep, where our children thrive, and where our children want to be. One might ask, "Are safe, vigorous, dynamic schools even a possibility in this day and age?" Such schools are not only possible but only need a bit of fine-tuning to correct their hidden dangers. I believe that healthy school climates can occur in all schools, public and private, large and small, wealthy and those on limited budgets.

Indeed, some successful schools already exist. Well, then, does this mean that there is already a perfect school that can be held up as a model for others to strive to emulate? The answer to this question is a definite *yes and no.* Yes, there are some dynamic healthy schools from which we can learn the necessary elements that make up such a climate, but because each school is unique, the model must be tailored to fit each school community.

We know that the changes must be based on solid research and that the overhaul process will take time and effort. However, we must keep in mind that even small improvements can have a significant impact on the school culture, which can lead to more substantial and permanent changes. Every thoughtful and well-planned change can move students and schools toward the realization of a vibrant school climate.

ESTABLISHING A FRAMEWORK

In Chapter 1, I ask the question, what can possibly be so original and work so successfully at some schools that students cannot wait to get there and experience a sense of community and shared responsibility, where learning is broad and deep? It's time to answer this question, with the development of an adaptable framework for schools to use to identify hidden dangers and to make the necessary changes.

Let's begin by restating our working definition of *school climate*. *School climate* refers to the unique combination of intellectual, behavioral, social, emotional, ethical/moral, and physical characteristics of the setting. In a healthy school climate, these six elements are in balance. Because all schools are dynamic places, it should be understood that these elements are in constant flux, but we strive to reach the optimal school climate, where these characteristics are in harmony. For these elements to be balanced, we need a solid foundation upon which we build our school climate. This foundation establishes that the basic needs of children will be the guiding principles upon which all policies and practices are built. These essential needs include

1. ongoing, nurturing relationships;
2. physical protection, safety, and regulation;
3. experiences tailored to individual differences;
4. developmentally appropriate experiences;
5. limit setting, structure, and expectations;
6. stable, supportive communities and cultural continuity; and
7. protecting the future—maintaining and supporting growth (Brazelton & Greenspan, 2000).

We have seen that many schools give only lip service to addressing these needs. Although some schools meet them better than others, there is room for improvement in all schools. So, the next building block in our foundation for a healthy school climate involves addressing the basic needs of children through an open-minded, nondefensive reflection of each school. The need for transparency in our educational systems is vital to overcoming these hidden dangers.

Transparency involves a process of reflection and flexibility that is free of intimidation, thus allowing for identification of problems. Hidden dangers can be identified, analyzed, and corrected in such a system in a straightforward manner. School personnel must be willing and capable of looking at established practices and beliefs from a multitude of perspectives.

When some students are not being well served, the policies and practices should readily be questioned and changed without all the red tape and excessive time, energy, and money that it currently takes to make an appropriate educational intervention. Most important, change needs to occur without further harm to the students and without the stress of lawyers in the schools. The political and ethical elements need to be rebalanced when policies and practices are in need of adjustment that affects all other elements within the school climate.

The third layer to our foundation involves creating an atmosphere of optimism. To do this, we need to turn our negative, pessimistic school environments into optimistic, flourishing places. The learning that we desire for our children cannot take place in such pessimistic atmospheres. For example, schools must begin to look for students' strengths and to believe and trust that most students want to learn and succeed. When schools teach optimism to their students, teachers, and staff, the climate projects a sense of hopefulness allowing for the self-reinforcing sense of optimism to become well established.

What was most striking about my research was the negative outlook perceived by parents and students in many of the schools. It was not until Scott and a few of the other students actually changed schools that they and their parents realized the differences between pessimistic and optimistic school climates.

Most of the issues mentioned by parents involved negative comments made by teachers, administrators, coaches, and even lunchroom staff. These negative comments, attitudes, and beliefs embody a disrespectful tone that no one should expect, even when visiting the IRS. Also, implied blame regarding learning and behavioral problems was placed on the student or on the family, as well as on the media. Certainly, these factors can contribute, but school professionals must acknowledge or at least ask what might be problematic within the schools that could be contributing to these issues. Professionals must ask, "What can we do differently to help this student learn?" Also, we must believe that there are ways to help, and we must not give in to the passivity of the times.

It was quite remarkable to listen and observe a total change in the tone of the students and parents when they spoke of the alternative school. Comments changed to a positive tone and included hopeful, controllable, workable solutions and situations. In the optimal schools, children were not being diagnosed; parents were not being blamed; and parents and children were listened to and helped to see that their input was valued. Children believed that they could have an impact, as well as some control and influence, on their learning. They felt unique and valued because the school's perspective appreciated their intelligences. Parents and children felt assured that they were emotionally safe and understood. They had found a sense of community within a school with a balanced climate.

The good news is that optimism can be learned. We need to teach our administrators, teachers, and students to become honestly optimistic, which involves a way of thinking that favors the environment in a positive manner, not a Pollyannaish manner. We can be both realistic and optimistic. In optimistic climates, teachers and students have choices and control of their teaching and learning within an approved healthy curriculum. Change is seen as a welcomed opportunity and red-tape procedures and codes are not necessary.

In an optimistic, positive climate, people will be viewed from the perspective of their strengths, not seen predominantly in terms of their weaknesses. Individual differences are valued, respected, indeed even celebrated in such climates. We become one as a community, respecting our uniqueness as human beings, all here for a unique purpose, while clearly understanding that we are all more alike than we are different. Yet, it is our very uniqueness that we must fully value if we are to deeply learn and understand one another. With such a climate, we are truly safer in our schools, in our communities, and such climates become self-fulfilling and sustainable.

This optimistic foundation leads us directly into the next essential foundation block: that of a strong, concerned, supportive administration with an open-door policy. It seems that all parents, educators, administrators, and even many of the children value schools with an open-door culture. School administrators must have the knowledge and skills to foster an open climate. Additionally, administrators and educators must be available and effective listeners. Student and parent concerns must be heard and addressed. So often, it appears that concerns are just dismissed, which tends to build anger.

Along these same lines the mission of the school clearly reflects its practices, and the practices and policies are based on solid research. Mission statements need to be regularly reviewed and updated, right along with the continual process of reviewing, analyzing, and updating policies and practices—all based on solid research.

The final building block of our optimal school climate involves the teachers, who are the most essential factor in our schools (right next to the students). Their importance cannot be overstated. We need teachers who are well educated and who receive ongoing meaningful training. Teachers should not be asked to handle more than they are credentialed and capable of managing, yet this is exactly what is happening in our schools. On any given day, teachers manage an array of problems. They need to be aware of and respect their limitations and call for professional assistance outside of the school without fear of reprimands. Specialized schools, educational consultants, and pediatricians can and should be utilized. These professionals, as well as alternative schooling options, can help resolve many problems for school officials and, most important, for the children experiencing distress. Teachers also must have high expectations for their students, and we must have high expectations for our teachers. We cannot expect teachers to teach at a level of excellence if they are being asking to baby-sit a variety of serious problems. There are situations that call for different interventions to help our children in need. Such interventions must be readily flexible, readily available, and agreeable to all involved.

Given a healthy, balanced school climate, I believe that most teachers are capable of doing outstanding work with our children. When teachers know and believe that they are truly doing good work with their students, then we will have teachers with high self-efficacy—an essential ingredient to a thriving school.

Along these same lines, we must understand that to get great teachers and to keep them teaching our children, we are going to have to pay them adequately. Teachers contribute more to our world than most other professions combined.

While we're on this issue of money, I should explain that research findings suggest that smaller classes do matter. However, this does not need to be a stumbling block for large urban schools. Many schools have successfully developed smaller communities within larger schools, each with its own identity. We must, however, work toward lowering the class size whenever possible, realizing that teachers can do a better job with more individualized attention with smaller groups.

> Teaching is the profession that teaches all other professions.
>
> —Unknown author

CONFRONTING THE ISSUES

In Chapter 3, I address the concealed damaging attitudes and assumptions. Our prime hidden danger is that we live in a nation of fear. This fear gets passed down to our children through many of our attitudes, assumptions, and procedures in the schools. We live in fear that our children will not get into the best preschools, that they will not get into Harvard, that they will not be able to keep up academically. We all want our children to be the best. This is only natural, but we have become so fearful of their well-being that many of the current practices are actually prohibiting successful academic progress.

As we could clearly see from case examples, oftentimes the attitudes, beliefs, and procedures that have become so ingrained in the schools just do not fit, explain, and help all children. Indeed, some of the practices actually cause problems for many children, thereby interfering with their learning. For example, the movement toward measuring, assessing, and accountability has both its positive and negative consequences, and it affects teachers' ability to focus on essential curriculum and causes significant problems for many children.

Additionally, we saw that some curriculum choices can be harmful. We can also see that we need to make additional curriculum changes for constructive change. For example, in the United States, we should foresee the need for education to focus on foreign-language acquisition. In a world as complex as ours, surely we can see the need for Americans to be able to understand and communicate with others from around the world; yet, this is not a serious focus in our schools. Clearly there are political, social, intellectual, behavioral, and even ethical implications here that cause the school climate to be out of balance.

Also, there is such a misguided academic push toward getting more and more time for learning so that necessities, such as recess, are being cut from the school day. This is not going to be helpful or healthy for children. It will negatively contribute to their obesity problem, and it will not help them gain skills. Doing more of what is already not working is not helpful. Kids need to get out, run around, clear their heads so that their academic time can be well used.

Sports are also a vital part of healthy growing. Sports should be accessible to all children. It is essential to keep sports in balance, too. The focus on competition, on winning at all costs, is dangerous. Pushing kids to win at the expense of learning to know their limits is harmful. Pushing kids to the point of injury is wrong and unethical. Pushing kids to run faster to the point that they vomit is wrong. Pushing kids to lose weight in order to wrestle, cheer, look better as a gymnast or skater is dangerous, unethical, even criminal. The violence we see in sports such as hockey, football, and even soccer is alarming. Such practices reinforce violent behavior, indeed even condone it. This is a dangerous practice. Finding a healthy balance with sports is essential.

Children also need to learn to eat healthy foods, in healthy amounts, and to pay attention to their individual nutritional needs. Each child is different; some children need to eat much more than others and eat more often. This should not be a problem when individual needs are respected. Children also need to learn to pay attention to their bodily signals, to understand their requirements for nourishment and other bodily functions. They need to learn about themselves just as much as they need to learn about math. This should be a natural process. By setting up hall passes and schedules for lunch where children have only 15–20 minutes to eat whatever they can does not set up a climate conducive to learning these necessary life skills. These hidden dangers set our kids up for eating disorders, including the serious crisis of obesity. It's easy to see the imbalance, with the physical, emotional, and basic needs not being met with these practices.

SYNTHESIS OF FOCUSED ISSUES

In Chapter 4, we looked at toxic testing practices that unfairly discriminate against numerous children, including those who may have learning differences, many boys (owing to gender differences in the classroom), students who may be out of sorts for a variety of reasons, students from various ethnic and cultural backgrounds, students from lower socioeconomic families, and children who do poorly on traditional measures. We are discriminating against some of the most talented and creative students—our truly inductive deep learners—with harmful testing approaches. We know that testing in and of itself is a neutral process. However, when testing is misused, it can become quite dangerous. Instead, testing needs to be used to demonstrate areas in which students need practice. Possibly, teaching approaches need to be modified; curriculum needs to be changed; or time needs to be given for more in-depth learning, such as that through experiential learning. Ultimately, testing should be composed of authentic assessment—including portfolio assessment, which can clearly demonstrate the learning and abilities of each student—and traditional forms of classroom testing and standardized testing, when used for the right reasons. Testing should never be used as a threat to students or teachers; as such, it is counterproductive. Misuse of testing puts the school climate out of balance intellectually and, most definitely, ethically. We must always keep in mind that testing should not be a harmful process. It should be a helpful and affirming process for the students and the teachers as well.

So, let's put together our new understanding of what is needed for testing to be helpful and nondangerous. First of all, additional research must be conducted on authentic assessment techniques. Although alternative approaches have been used to assess students for many years, there is little well-done research, including longitudinal studies, to demonstrate the effectiveness of such approaches. But this is true with conventional tests as well; studies done on more traditional testing approaches have not shown the damage inflicted on many students, because of the type of research conducted. Each student becomes a statistic, and we cannot see the damaging effects and the reasons for these results—only that some students perform poorly. Computers allow us to crunch large numbers and come up with scores. However, it is imperative that those interpreting these numbers know the numbers' limitations and, most important, how to help each student demonstrate his or her unique gifts, as well as address those areas that need more intensive instruction.

In Chapter 5, we saw the damaging effects of labeling. Diagnosis does not belong in the schools; it needs to stay in the hands of our medical and psychological professionals. Teachers do not need a diagnosis to teach a child appropriately. They do need to know how to assess children for their strengths as well as their weaknesses and to appropriately interpret assessment measures to individualize an appropriate teaching strategy. Believe it or not, teachers receive very little training in the art and skills of assessment and testing. Undergraduate educational curriculums are so tied up with meeting the nonessential goals established by the state and federal guidelines that essential knowledge and skills are not well addressed as part of teacher training. Children also should be asked what might help them. So often, input from the child is seen as being pointless, yet they are the true experts on themselves. Furthermore, to consult with the children gives them a sense of control and responsibility for their learning. We must listen to our children. Here again, we can see the negative impact of political policies that throw off the balance in our schools.

The increase in labeling and the diagnosis of disorders were also addressed in Chapter 5. It appears that this increase involves the need to label somewhat quirky, bright kids who are poorly served within the traditional educational system. By labeling these children, schools get more money for funding, which so very often gets handed right over to the lawyers who should not be in the schools — at least not as often as they currently are. Lawyers may argue that it is a result of law suits that change occurs, but in few cases is this accurate. Certainly, cases such as *Brown vs. Board of Education* have been life changing for many students. However, the day-to-day cases do nothing but take time and money away from needed programs and make the lawyers richer. We can and need to use this educational money more effectively. It seems obvious that children's individual needs are not being met in many instances, that individual differences are not being respected, and that the balance within the school climate is being disrupted in several areas, including ethical areas.

Labels can also interfere with children socially, behaviorally, intellectually, and psychologically.

In Chapter 6, I address the hidden dangers of unintentional gender inequity in our schools. Again, here we have seen problems with meeting the individual needs of children (male and female) and not addressing their unique differences in terms of development. Boys and girls develop differently, not just in the obvious physical ways but in their cognitive abilities as well. Boys and girls may well need to learn different curricula, in a different manner, at different times. We saw the gender divide in our schools from research and in case studies. Clearly, we can see that there are gender issues that need to be addressed. The causes of these gender discrepancies are multifaceted and involve society's perceptions of boys, educational expectations, new state and federal testing policies, school climate, psychological and emotional differences, and brain-based and biological differences (Gunzelmann & Connell, 2006).

Let's take a closer look at what can be done to help establish a healthier school climate for the gender issues. First of all, we need to confront our understanding of boys and girls and their unique strengths and needs. Second, we need to become accepting of individual differences; it may be accurate to say that more boys than girls have difficulty sitting still and coloring within the lines, but it can be damaging to see only the typical scenarios and to stereotype. We must fully understand the uniqueness of each child. Boys and girls should be assisted in understanding that we all learn differently and that our learning should be based on all of our unique contributions to the learning environment, not on competition and who can color the neatest or do their math facts the fastest.

We also need to help all children, regardless of gender, to develop real friendships and to transcend the cliques that are based on popularity and not a true sense of companionship and caring. Along these same lines, students need to be taught problem-solving approaches to acquiring social skills and to understanding one another. Boys should not be pushed to grow up too fast. They should be understood as having needs similar to those of girls, for nurturing and close, caring relationships, particularly at times when they most need it, into their teen years and older. All issues of diversity must be handled in a manner that provides an optimal learning environment for all students, apart from gender, race, socioeconomic level, and any other factor that may affect the learning of the child. The issues discussed in Chapter 6 can put the school climate out of balance by not appropriately addressing children's basic needs for individualized instruction based on developmental levels and by not setting an atmosphere that is helpful for boys, who may experience difficulties socially, behaviorally, and intellectually. Clearly, there are ethical issues when a school does not address gender discrepancies.

In Chapter 7, I address issues of safety policies (including zero tolerance and lockdowns) and issues of school-related violence (including bullying and cliques). It appears that the atmosphere in the schools is one of anxiety and heightened vigilance related to the fear that has taken over our nation. The schools themselves have played right into this hysteria. It will not be until we look at schools as places that are to be child focused, not Big Brother focused—places where children can be playful, be inquisitive, truly be children again—that we will see many forms of school violence subside.

It seems that school policies reflect an attitude of distrust toward our children, not expecting them to behave appropriately. These policies expect kids to act out, to bully others, and to be violent. This expectation can become the norm if we are not careful. If children begin to believe that violence is anticipated, then such behavior may become typical, normal in the eyes of our children. They will become desensitized to the cruelty in our society.

The media already do much too much in desensitizing our children regarding violent behavior. Certainly, we do not want our schools unintentionally playing into this process. The money, time, and effort spent on preparing for catastrophe is a real danger that focuses our children into believing that they are not safe. These issues can put our children's basic needs at risk, along with making the school climate's social, ethical, intellectual, emotional, and behavioral areas out of balance as well.

In Chapter 8, I take a closer look at problems within the physical school buildings, which can be quite unsafe and disruptive to the well-being and education of our children and our school personnel as well. Our older school buildings should meet basic safety guidelines for air quality, water quality, and building codes. Additionally, the land and materials used for building, remodeling, and renovations need to be chosen with the long-term well-being of our children and all school personnel in mind.

Green building practices should be utilized whenever possible (see Northeast Sustainable Energy Association, 2001; U.S. Environmental Protection Agency, 2007c). Green schools are often called *high-performance schools* because they use safe, natural materials and operate in an efficient and ecological manner (see U.S. Environmental Protection Agency, 2007d). Furthermore, green schools "protect occupant health, provide a productive learning environment, connect students to the natural world, increase average daily attendance, reduce operating costs, improve teacher satisfaction and retention, and reduce overall impact to the environment" (Global Green USA, 2006, para. 1).

Classroom design and organization must also be considered. Why not have a classroom without desks or, at the very least, one where children are not so restricted by rules about staying in their seats? Children need to get up and move around. Students in such settings are happier and healthier. Researchers at the Mayo Clinic believe that such classrooms will engage our future schools (Mayo Clinic, 2006b). Furthermore, furniture should be comfortable and moveable to accommodate changing needs.

Even with routine maintenance of our schools, we must monitor and adopt the least toxic approach. Hazardous chemicals, including those used for cleaning and pest management, should be eliminated. Parents and school personnel should be informed of any chemicals being used and where and when applications are taking place. Unnecessary use of harmful chemicals should not be used merely for aesthetic reasons, such as lawn care or for any other unnecessary usage.

All schools, whether old or new, should undergo regular professional monitoring for all potentially harmful issues. The results should be researched, analyzed, and changes should be made, as they should with all dangers in the schools. Any necessary changes should be made by professionals trained to handle such problems. This area fits under basic needs, but it also affects the physical and ethical areas, unbalancing the entire climate for all students and school personnel.

So, in a nutshell, an optimal, healthy, and safe school climate, free from hidden dangers, can be diagramed as such (see Figure 9.1). In a safe and healthy school climate, we see choices, balance, alternatives, and a belief in the inherent goodness of people to want to do their best work when the circumstances support self-actualizing be-

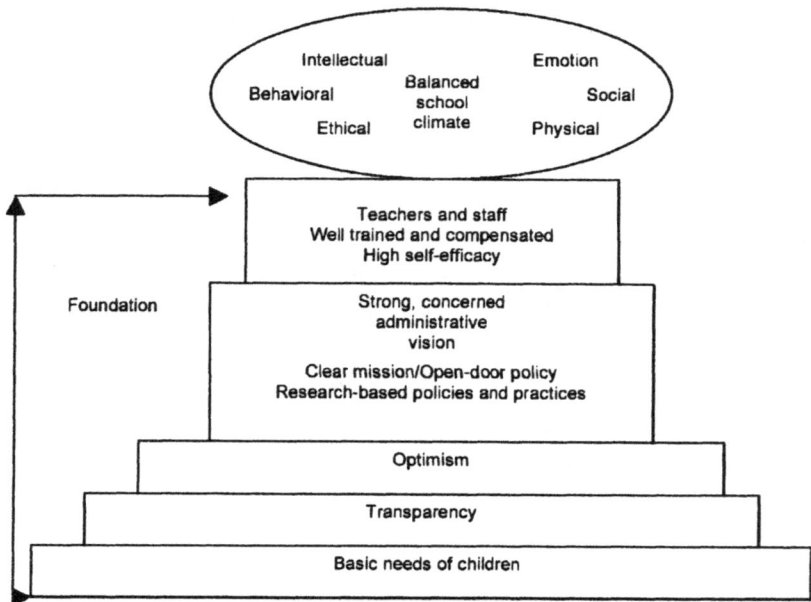

Figure 9.1.   A School Free of Hidden Dangers: A Balanced School Climate

havior. Children want to go to school; they experience a sense of belonging and achievement. All aspects of the school climate seem to be in reasonable balance (intellectually, socially, emotionally, behaviorally, physically, and ethically). Children's most basic needs are met in an optimistic atmosphere.

School is a large part of our lives and the lives of our children. It should be a place that we all want to go and spend our time, where we feel valued and appreciated. As such, the school offers an optimal learning climate, a climate and a sense of belonging that even the most difficult circumstances outside the school cannot break down. The school, being free from hidden dangers, offers a way to have a real impact on our youth, despite the current problems that we are seeing in our culture. Let's see how we can transcend these hidden dangers and keep our schools thriving, safe, and self-reinforcing.

> The culture may advertise its famous melting pot slogan, but everyone knows the true melting pot is the classroom and playground, where every variety of integration of turf and difference, not to mention every dynamic of the lower brain stem and cerebral cortex, has to be worked out.
>
> —Tom Cottle (2004)

CHAPTER 10

Transcending Hidden Dangers for All Children

It's time to transcend the hidden dangers in our schools. We know what we need for the climate of all schools to be free of hidden dangers, but how do we implement these identified necessities and how do we maintain an optimal school climate without falling back into the hidden-dangers vicious cycle? To transcend the hidden-dangers trap, we need to break the negative vicious cycle and generate a positive, dynamic, and self-sustaining cycle of reflection, research, analysis, and change.

I do believe that at the heart of most schools, there are concerned administrators and teachers. Most of our school faculty and employees want to make a positive contribution to the lives of our children, but they get bogged down in red tape and long-established approaches. Administrators, teachers, parents, children, and community members must work together to reflect on the hidden issues within their schools, carefully gathering and reviewing the related research, analyzing, then making needed changes, and regularly reflecting and revising when necessary—it will truly be a self-sustaining cycle.

Now, we have a plan for a balanced, self-reinforcing, sustainable, optimal, and safe school climate, and we can make it a reality for all children. We can now make our schools places where children and teachers thrive from the excitement and challenge that true learning inspires. Figure 10.1 shows us that we can transcend the hidden dangers within schools by creating dynamic, self-sustaining cycles linking reflection, research, analysis, and change.

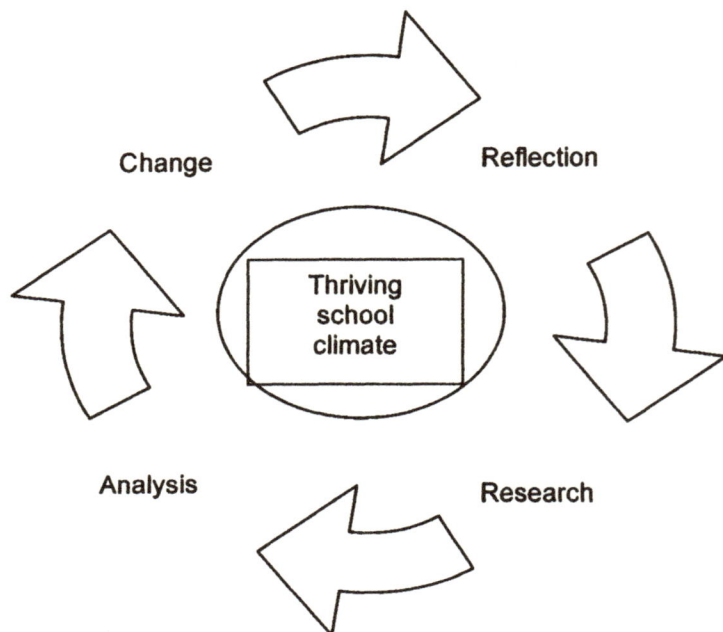

Figure 10.1.   A Dynamic, Self-Sustaining Cycle for Thriving Schools for All Children

IN THE INTERIM

Schools can and will change. We have many dedicated, hard-working, well-intentioned professionals in our schools. But change takes time; sometimes, it takes longer than we can wait, particularly if it is our child who is suffering. Therefore, we need to be able to make necessary, immediate interventions for some children, possibly changing classrooms, changing approaches within classrooms, or even changing to a different school may be warranted. Options without a lot of red tape and labeling need to be available. We need to support our educational institutions, awakening our educators to view problems within our schools from a different perspective, by redesigning our schools from the foundations of the buildings to the core of the educational process in many of our schools.

It's going to take time, research, effort, and courage to challenge current educational systems plagued by hidden dangers. We know from history that educational institutions are among the slowest to change. There is no doubt that we need to begin this process. However, in the meantime, there are many children who are caught up in the fallout from hidden dangers, and change may not come soon enough. Their futures are at risk. Many children will not attain the skills needed to become who they are capable of becoming if we do not help them to obtain an education free of hidden dangers. So, as we begin the process of correcting the problems inherent in our schools, we need to assist our children with transcending the immediate hidden dangers so that no further harm is done to any child.

All children deserve both a chance to revive their desire to learn and an opportunity to attend schools that are free from hidden, self-defeating problems. We all have encountered youth who do not care about their education, who have so many problems—poverty, homelessness, family, and societal problems. It's understandable that academic issues may not be first on the list of priorities for these children. Yet, if we can make our schools safe, desirable places, we can help these students transcend their most difficult life challenges.

We can and must make schools places free from hidden dangers that impede the development of a vibrant school climate and thus immunize them from harmful outside influences. And so we allow and encourage them to grow, learn, and cope with difficulties in a manner that will enable them to successfully negotiate our complex society and to contribute, when they are grown and ready, in a positive manner to the next generation. We cannot afford to lose a significant part of our younger generation to the apathy that we are seeing in our schools, a reflection of the larger society.

We must help all students transcend these hidden dangers, to reconnect their interest in learning, their creativity, and their belief in themselves to be able to do great things. We need to believe in our children and to be strong enough not to let these hidden dangers overpower our children's desire to learn. We must realize that the cases presented here are of children who were seen as the problems.

Yet, most of them had no diagnoses of learning disabilities, attention problems, or primary psychological disorders. These were children who were poorly understood and most definitely underserved by their schools. We can clearly see that the children were not the problem; however, certain school policies, practices, and societal beliefs contribute to the educational crisis.

In turn, parents and teachers were blaming their kids, thus compounding the children's difficulties. I do believe that these dangers are in part related to the increase in depression, anxiety, and other disorders that we are seeing with our youth. These kids cannot wait for our schools to improve their climates. They need change now. In the meantime, while we await these constructive educational changes, we need options for our children. During these times, it is important to know that we have choices, that we can turn to other resources, including alternative education approaches: charter schools, free schools, home schooling, e-schooling, and a variety of hybrid educational approaches. Sometimes, it takes an immediate change to save a child from a toxic school climate. In some cases, all it takes is a change to a school that fits the child. Children such as Scott, Nicholas, Adam, Sally, Luke, and all the children of the cases that we have seen deserve our help. Oftentimes, all we need to help these students transcend the hidden dangers is a change in approach or even a change in school. Choices and options are essential to transcending the hidden dangers in schools.

A variety of schools and approaches should be available to all children. A one-size-fits-all approach can no longer be tolerated by parents and teachers. There are too many children who are being compromised, being robbed of developing their potential to the fullest, being prevented from becoming who they were meant to be. Advances in technology afford us many unique opportunities to meet the needs of all students. For example, in a case presented earlier, Scott discovered that he did much better when allowed to take computerized versions of traditional tests. Other technological advances have allowed us to work with e-portfolios and their many added benefits. Storage of materials is much easier; many reviewers can assess students' material online for a complete evaluation; and students can do the work of preparing and presenting their own portfolios, thus cutting the cost and time required to do other forms of assessment.

Alternative approaches to education are becoming available because of technological advances, including e-schooling and a variety of hybrid forms of distance learning. These options open alternative educational possibilities to all children—children such as Sally and Carol—but also children in the most remote areas of the world where teachers and schools may not be available. Each child is unique, and we must approach each child with respect, caring, and awe. We have a lot to learn from each child. Let's help these kids become who they were meant to be by getting rid of these hidden dangers in our schools.

Teachers, too, must have options and choices to rise above the inherent problems in schools. There are too many teachers who lose their idealism after their first few years of teaching; they give up trying to make the impact that they intended. Alternative education approaches empower our teachers, reawakening their desire, their passion, that sent many of our best teachers into the field in the first place. We cannot sit idly by any longer and allow this to occur. Teachers can make a difference starting today. Small changes within one's classroom can make all the difference in the world to a child who is floundering. Teachers can begin by making little changes within their classrooms while the administrators are attempting to make larger-scale changes within their schools. To transcend these hidden dangers within our schools, we need to continue to conduct well-planned research within our schools and to keep up with the cutting-edge research on children from a multidisciplinary perspective. Most important, we need to be outspoken when we see things in our schools that are troubling, even when that's how things have always been done or when it goes against the grain of public policy. To do our best work, to help our children thrive, we must not tolerate mediocre education; we need choices for our children and teachers now. These choices must be made readily available for all students, and they must be free of stigma and labels. Such alternatives must be fully supported by our school personnel and seen as respected options to meet the needs of all students.

A MESSAGE TO THOSE CONFRONTING
HIDDEN DANGERS IN OUR SCHOOLS

I want to conclude with a message to all those affected by the problems in our schools, to help us transcend these hidden dangers:

To parents: Believe in your child. Remember those hopes and dreams that you had for him or her at the time of birth. A lot has happened since then. He's been exposed to the toxicity of our society, to the dangers within the very schools that are supposed to nurture, protect, and teach him. She has learned to doubt herself—her curious nature has been suppressed so that she has become a passive student, not the vibrant little child you once knew. Remember and believe that your child can get back that innate love of learning. Your child needs your support now just as he or she did as an infant, maybe even more so.

To teachers: Remember when you first wanted to be a teacher? You wanted to help children love to learn. Possibly, you wanted to protect some children from the pain and problems that you experienced when you were a student. We can make our schools and our classrooms places where children can learn and thrive without adding to their many burdens. But as teachers, we cannot give up; we must help the children learn to be optimistic, to be resilient, and to transcend these issues. Schools can be places that allow and even encourage children to thrive, a haven away from toxic conditions. In establishing such a positive climate, you will be allowing yourself to thrive as a teacher, making the very contribution that you were meant to make. Transcend the ordinary approaches; question current practices and beliefs; have the courage to change what is not working, what is harming many children.

To children: Never, ever doubt your abilities. You are unique. Some things are difficult to learn. But if you don't get discouraged and you learn about yourself, valuing your uniqueness, you will find a way in which you learn best, a way in which you can express your achievements, a way to learn what you need in order to be who you are supposed to be—to discover your purpose and reason for being. And most important, don't be afraid to ask for help from more than one person. Find people who value you; they may not fully understand you at the moment, but if they believe in you, over time they will find a way to help you get the schooling that is right for you.

The final, most important message: I firmly believe that most teachers, school administrators, psychologists, and parents are trying to do a good job, but at times they revert to the most typical, although faulty, pattern of thinking and behavior because it is familiar, because it is how it always has been done. Don't get caught in the hidden-dangers trap.

HOPE FOR THE FUTURE

There is hope for the future of our schools, for our children, for our communities, and for the larger community of global citizens. Identifying hidden dangers includes looking at our fears and preconceived notions about unfamiliar ways of thinking. We have much to learn from one another. All we need do is look into the eyes of the children to see their desire to learn, succeed, and understand each other. We need to reach out to all the children around the world, to connect via the link of worldwide learning through a healthy, global, educational climate. We have so much to offer one another, to learn the customs and cultures of others, to share our knowledge with others, to advance because of their knowledge, and to stimulate new ideas for the benefit of all. We have the technology to reach out to all children around the world, even those in the most remote areas, to allow all to benefit from education. Through education, we may finally understand that although we are unique individuals, we are truly more alike than we are different. Working together, we can achieve greater accomplishments than we can if we work apart. Global education holds the key to a peaceful future and so transcends all our hidden dangers.

Naturally, it's not all in the book. It's going to take time, research, effort, and courage to challenge the current toxic educational systems, but it is our most important national concern. The hidden dangers are the real dangers that we must confront to allow our children to prosper.

For all those who want to help our children transcend the hidden dangers . . .

What Children Need
Listen to your children;
For they need to tell you of the troubles that they encounter every day.
Hear the unspoken words underneath their anger and frustration.
Watch your children;
For they need to show you what it's like to be misunderstood.
See the hurt in their anxious and withdrawn behavior.
Appreciate your children;
For they need to succeed, but doubt themselves.
Know that they are capable if guided with care and patience.
Remember what it was like when you were young;
For the children need to learn from our experiences.
Understand too, that it is different now; the pressures and problems are more complex.
Share your mistakes and struggles with your children,
So they need not feel so alone.
Offer them support and understanding.
Model responsible behavior for your children;
Because they need to learn to be conscientious too.
Support their hard work and persistence.
Value the uniqueness of your children;
Because they need to learn to understand themselves and others.
Appreciate the diversity of all, while knowing we are really more alike than different.
Be there for your children;
For they need you now more than ever.
Take time to let them know they are respected and understood.
Believe in your children;
Because they need to believe in themselves and have hope for the future.
Instill a sense of confidence, love, and community so they will do the same for others.

References

Aiken, L. R. (2000). *Psychological testing and assessment.* Boston: Allyn & Bacon.

American Bar Association. (2000). *Juvenile justice policies: Zero tolerance policy report.* Chicago: Author.

American Psychiatric Association. (2000). *Diagnostic and statistical manual of mental disorders* (4th ed., text rev.). Washington, DC: Author.

AspergerResources.com. (n.d.). *Famous people with Asperger's syndrome.* Retrieved May 16, 2007, from www.aspergerresources.com/famous_people_with_aspergers.html

Ayers, W., Dohrn, B., & Ayers, R. (Eds.). (2001). *Zero tolerance: Resisting the drive for punishment in our schools.* New York: New Press.

Bandura, A. (1965). Influence of models' reinforcement contingencies on the acquisition of imitative responses. *Journal of Personality and Social Psychology, 1,* 589–595.

Bandura, A. (1977). *Social learning theory.* New York: General Learning Press.

Baron-Cohen, S. (2003). *The essential difference: The truth about the male and female brain.* New York: Basic Books.

Biederman, J., Mick, E., Faraone, S. V., Braaten, E., Doyle, A., Spencer, T., et al. (2002). Influence of gender on attention deficit/hyperactivity disorder in children referred to a psychiatric clinic. *American Journal of Psychiatry, 159,* 36–42.

Biederman, J., Newcorn, J., & Sprich, S. (1991). Comorbidity of attention-deficit/hyperactivity disorder with conduct, depressive, anxiety, and other disorders. *American Journal of Psychiatry, 148,* 564–577.

Black, S. (2004). Safe schools don't need zero tolerance. *Education Digest, 70*(2), 27–31.

Boys Project. (n.d.). *The Boys Project: Helping boys become successful men.* Retrieved July 11, 2007, from www.boysproject.net/

BrainyQuote.com. (2007). *Robert Sternberg quotes*. Retrieved January 10, 2007, from www.brainyquote.com/quotes/authors/r/robert_sternberg.html

Brazelton, T. B., & Greenspan, S. I. (2000). *The irreducible needs of children: What every child must have to grow, learn, and flourish*. Cambridge, MA: Perseus.

Center for Disease Control, National Center for Health Statistics. (2005). *Asthma Prevalence, Health Care Use and Mortality, 2002*. Retrieved July 15, 2007, from www.cdc.gov/nchs/products/pubs/pubd/hestats/asthma/asthma.htm

Children's Environmental Health Network. (2005, September 5). *A childsafe U.S. chemicals policy*. Washington, DC: Author. Available at www.cehn.org

Clinton, H. (2000, April 6). *New York Times*. Retrieved August 22, 2007, from www.ontheissues.org/2008/Hillary_Clinton_Education.htm.

Collins, M. (1996). *Documented on CBS "60 Minutes."* Retrieved January 10, 2007, from www.enthink.com/quotations/teachers_and_teaching/

Conlin, M. (2003, May 26). The new gender gap. *Business Week*, 74–82.

Connell, D. (2002). Left brain/right brain. *Instructor, 112*(2), 28–32.

Connell, D., & Gunzelmann, B. (2004). The new gender gap: Why are so many boys floundering while so many girls are soaring? *Instructor, 113*(6), 14–17.

Consumer Product Safety Commission. (2000, June 13). *News from CPSC: CPSC releases test results on crayons: Industry to reformulate* (Release No. 00–123). Washington, DC: Office of Information and Public Affairs. Retrieved May 29, 2007, from www.cpsc.gov/CPSCPUB/PREREL/prhtm l00/00123.html

Coopersmith, S. (1967). *The antecedent of self-esteem*. San Franscico: Freeman.

Cottle, T. (2004). Feeling scared. *Educational Horizons, 83*(1), 42–54.

Elkind, D. (2001). *The hurried child* (3rd ed.). Cambridge, MA: DeCapo Press.

Farberman, R. (2006). Zero tolerance policies can have unintended effects, APA report finds. *Monitor on Psychology, 37*(9), 27.

Gardner, H. (1991). *The unschooled mind: How children think and how schools should teach*. New York: Basic Books.

Gardner, H. (1999). *Intelligence reframed: Multiple intelligences for the 21st century*. New York: Basic Books.

Gardner, H., Csikszentmihalyi, M., & Damon, W. (2001). *Good work: When excellence and ethics meet.* New York: Basic Books.

Gates, B. (2005, February 26). *National Governors Association/Achieve Summit: Prepared remarks.* Retrieved May 28, 2007, from www.nga .org/cda/files/ES05GATES.pdf

Giroux, H. A. (2003). Racial injustice and disposable youth in the age of zero tolerance. *Qualitative Studies in Education, 16*(4), 553–565.

Glew, G., Fan, M., Katon, W., Rivara, F., & Kernic, M. (2005). Bullies, victims, and their feelings about school. *Archives of Pediatrics and Adolescent Medicine, 159*(11), 1004–1085.

Global Green USA. (2006). *Green Schools Initiative.* Retrieved May 31, 2007, from www.globalgreen.org/greenbuilding/GreenSchools.html

Gunzelmann, B. (2004). Hidden dangers within our schools: What are these safety problems and how can we fix them? *Educational Horizons, 83*(1), 66–76.

Gunzelmann, B. (2005). Toxic testing: It's time to reflect upon our current testing practices. *Educational Horizons, 83*(3), 212–220.

Gunzelmann, B., & Connell, D. (2006). The new gender gap: Social, psychological, and educational perspectives. *Educational Horizons, 84*(2), 94–101.

Gurian, M. (2001). *Boys and girls learn differently! A guide for teachers and parents.* San Francisco: Jossey-Bass.

Harvard University, Civil Rights Project. (2001). *Opportunities suspended: The devastating consequences of zero tolerance and school discipline.* Retrieved May 30, 2007, from www.civilrightsproject.harvard.edu/ convenings/zerotolerance/synopsis.php

Harvard University, Civil Rights Project. (2003). *Minority children with disabilities will be harmed in disproportionate numbers if IDEA's discipline safeguards are reduced or eliminated.* Retrieved May 30, 2007, from www.civilrightsproject.harvard.edu/policy/alerts/idea.php

Hirsch, E. D. (1996). *The schools we need and why we don't have them.* New York: Doubleday.

Hirsch, E. D. (2006). *The knowledge deficit: Closing the shocking education gap for American children.* New York: Houghton Mifflin.

Hoffmann, B. (1962). *The tyranny of testing.* New York: Macmillan.

Hoy, W. K., Tarter, C. J., & Bliss, J. (1990). Organizational climate, school health, and effectiveness: A comparative analysis. *Educational Administration Quarterly, 26*(3), 260–279.

Hoy, W. K., Tarter, C. J., & Kottkamp, R. B. (1991). *Open schools/healthy schools: Measuring organizational climate.* Newbury Park, CA: Sage.

Hoy, W. K., & Woolfolk, A. E. (1993). Teacher's sense of efficacy and the organizational health of schools. *Elementary School Journal, 93*(4), 355–372.

Hoyle, J. R., & Slater, R. O. (2001). Searching for accountability for a loving school environment. *Phi Delta Kappa, 82,* 790–794.

IllinoisLoop.org. (2006a). Boys and girls. In *Quotes on education.* Retrieved January 10, 2007, from www.illinoisloop.org/quotes.html# gender

IllinoisLoop.org. (2006b). Education: Theory and practice. In *Quotes on education.* Retrieved May 21, 2007, from www.illinoisloop.org/quotes .html#educationtheory

IllinoisLoop.org. (2006c). What Americans think about schools. In *Quotes on education.* Retrieved May 31, 2007, from www.illinoisloop.org/ quotes.html#survey

Kids Health. (2005, August). *Coping with cliques.* Retrieved May 18, 2007, from www.kidshealth.org/teen/your mind/problems/cliques.html

Kids Health. (2006, June). *Lead poisioning.* Retrieved July 15, 2007, from www.kidshealth.org/parent/medical/brain/lead_poisioning.html

Kindlon, D., & Thompson, M. (2000). *Raising Cain: Protecting the emotional life of boys.* New York: Ballantine.

Koch, K. (2000, March 10). Zero tolerance for school violence. *CQ Researcher, 10,* 185–208. Retrieved May 30, 2007, from http://library.cq-press.com/cqresearcher/cqresrre2000031000

Kohn, A. (2000). *The case against standardized testing: Raising scores, ruining the schools.* Portsmouth, NH: Heinemann.

Kohn, A. (2004). Safety from the inside out: Rethinking traditional approaches. *Educational Horizons, 83*(1), 33–41.

Kozol, J. (1991). *Savage inequalities.* New York: Crown.

Levine, M. (2002). *A mind at a time.* New York: Simon & Schuster.

Mayo Clinic. (2006a). *Childhood obesity.* Retrieved January 30, 2007, from www.mayoclinic.com/health/childhood

Mayo Clinic. (2006b). *Classroom of the future.* Retrieved January 30, 2007, from www.mayoclinic.org/levine-classroom-future/1

McEvoy, A., & Welker, R. (2000). Antisocial behavior, academic failure, and school climate: A critical review. *Journal of Emotional and Behavioral Disorders, 8*(3), 130.

Meier, D. (2002). *In schools we trust: Creating communities of learning in an era of testing and standardization.* Boston: Beacon Press.

Meier, D. (2004). For safety's sake. *Educational Horizons, 83*(1), 55–60.

Merrow, J. (2001). *Choosing excellence: "Good enough" schools are not good enough.* Lanham, MD: Scarecrow Press.

Merrow, J. (2004). Safety and excellence. *Educational Horizons, 83*(1), 19–32.

Mosca, F. J., & Hollister, A. (2004). External control and zero tolerance: Is fear of our youth driving these policies? [Book review]. *Educational Horizons, 83*(1), 2–5.

National Center for Education Statistics. (1998). *The condition of education.* Washington, DC: U.S. Department of Education.

National Clearinghouse for Educational Facilities. (2007a). *Resource lists: Color theory for classrooms and schools.* Retrieved May 20, 2007, from www.edfacilities.org/rl/color.cfm

National Clearinghouse for Educational Facilities. (2007b). *Resource lists: Mold in schools.* Retrieved May 20, 2007, from www.edfacilities.org/rl/Mold.cfm

National Clearinghouse for Educational Facilities. (2007c). *Resource lists: School cleaning and maintenance practices.* Retrieved May 20, 2007, from www.edfacilities.org/rl/cleaning.cfm

National Institute of Environmental Health Services. (2006, May). *Asthma and its environmental triggers.* Retrieved May 30, 2007, from www.niehs.nih.gov/oc/factsheets/pdf/asthma.pdf

National Institutes of Health. (2001, May 3). *NHLBI reports new asthma data for World Asthma Day 2001: Asthma still a problem but more groups fighting it.* Retrieved May 20, 2007, from www.nih.gov/news/pr/may2001/nhlbi-03.htm

National Sleep Foundation. (2007). *How much sleep is enough?* Retrieved August 14, 2007, from www.sleepfoundation.org/site/c.huIXKjM0IxF/b.2419131/k.6C23/How_Much_Sleep_Is_Enough.htm

Natural Resources Defense Council. (2000). *Lead paint in schools.* Retrieved July 15, 2007, from www.nrdc.org/health/kids/qleadsch.asp#problem

Newberger, E. H. (1999). *The men they will become: The nature and nurture of the male character.* Cambridge, MA: Perseus.

Noonan, J. (2004). School climate and the safe school: Seven contributing factors. *Educational Horizons, 83*(1), 61–65.

Noonan, M. J. (2007). Personal communication.

Nordenberg, T. (1998). *Miracle drugs vs. superbugs: Preserving the use of antibiotics.* Rockville, MD: U.S. Food and Drug Administration. Retrieved May 18, 2007, from www.fda.gov/fdac/features/1998/698_bugs .html

Northeast Sustainable Energy Association. (2001). *Building green schools resource list.* Retrieved January 30, 2007, from www.nesea.org/buildings/ greenschoolsresources.html

PBS.org. (2007). *Zero tolerance.* Retrieved May 29, 2007, from www.pbs.org/newshour/extra/features/july-dec99/zerotolerance.html

Peterson, R. L., & Skiba, R. (2001). Creating school climates that prevent school violence. *Clearinghouse, 74*(3), 155–163.

Pollack, W. (1998). *Real boys: Rescuing our sons from the myths of boyhood.* New York: Holt.

Popham, W. J. (1999). Why standardized tests don't measure educational quality. *Using Standards and Assessment, 56*(6), 8–15.

Population Reference Bureau. (1999, February). *Reports on America.* Retrieved May 31, 2007, from www.prb.org/Source/ReportonAmerica 2000CensusChallenge.pdf

Rose, L. C. (2004). No Child Left Behind: The mathematics of guaranteed failure. *Educational Horizons, 82*(2), 121–130.

Saltman, K. J., & Gabbard, D. (Eds.) (2003). *Education as enforcement: The militarization in our schools.* New York: RoutledgeFalmer.

Santilli, J. (2002). Health effects of mold exposure in schools. *Current Allergy and Asthma Reports, 2,* 460–467.

Schneider, A., & Smith, C. (2000, May 23). Major brands of kids' crayons contain asbestos, tests show. *Seattle Post-Intelligencer.* Retrieved May 31, 2007, from http://seattlepi.nwsource.com/national/cray23.shtml

Schultz, D. P., & Schultz, S. E. (2001). *Theories of personality.* Belmont, CA: Wadsworth.

Seligman, M. (1995). *The optimistic child: A revolutionary program to safeguard children from depression and build lifelong resilience.* New York: Houghton Mifflin.

Seligman, M. (1998). *Learned optimism.* New York: Pocket Books.

Sizer, T. R., & Sizer, N. F. (1999). *The students are watching: Schools and the moral contract.* Boston: Beacon Press.

Springer, S., & Deutsch, G. (1998). *Left brain, right brain—Perspectives from cognitive neuroscience* (5th ed.). New York: Freeman.

Tirozzi, G. N., & Uro. G. (1997). Education reform in the United States: National policy in support of local efforts for school improvement. *American Psychologist, 52*(3), 241–249.

U.S. Census Bureau. (2000). *2006 population estimates.* Retrieved May 21, 2007, from http://factfinder.census.gov/servlet/SAFFPopulation?_submenu Id=population_0&sse=on

U.S. Department of Education. (2004). *The Elementary and Secondary Education Act (the No Child Left Behind Act of 2001).* Retrieved May 7, 2007, from www.ed.gov/policy/elsec/leg/esea02/index.html

U.S. Department of Education Planning and Evaluation Service. (2006). *Archived: International activities.* Retrieved May 31, 2007, from www .ed.gov/offices/OUS/PES/int_activities.html#assessments

U.S. Environmental Protection Agency. (1989, March). *Recognition and management of pesticide poisonings.* Retrieved May 20, 2007, from www.epa.gov/pesticides/safety/healthcare/handbook/handbook.pdf EPA 735–R-98–003.

U.S. Environmental Protection Agency. (1992, June). *Healthy lawn, healthy environment.* Retrieved May 20, 2007, from www.epa.gov/oppfead1/ Publications/lawncare.pdf

U.S. Environmental Protection Agency. (1994). *Reducing radon in the schools: A team approach* (EPA Report No. 402-R-94-008). Washington, DC: Author.

U.S. Environmental Protection Agency. (2002, January). *Protecting children from pesticides.* Retrieved May 20, 2007, from www.epa.gov/ pesticides/factsheets/kidpesticide.htm

U.S. Environmental Protection Agency. (2007a). *Asbestos in schools.* Retrieved May 20, 2007, from www.epa.gov/asbestos/pubs/schools.html

U.S. Environmental Protection Agency. (2007b). *Brownfields cleanup and redevelopment.* Retrieved May 27, 2007, from www.epa.gov/swerosps/ bf/

U.S. Environmental Protection Agency. (2007c). *Green indoor environments.* Retrieved May 27, 2007, from www.epa.gov/iaq/greenbuilding/ index.html

U.S. Environmental Protection Agency. (2007d). *High performance schools.* Retrieved May 27, 2007, from www.epa.gov/iaq/schooldesign/ highperformance.html

U.S. Environmental Protection Agency. (2007e). *Mold remediation in schools and commercial buildings.* Retrieved January 30, 2007, from www.epa.gov/iaq/molds/mold_remediation.html

U.S. Environmental Protection Agency. (2007f). *Radon in schools* (2nd ed.). Retrieved May 21, 2007, from www.epa.gov/radon/pubs/schoolrn .html

U.S. General Accounting Office. (1996). *Indoor air quality. School facilities: America's schools report differing conditions* (GAO Report No. HEHS-96-103). Retrieved May 20, 2007, from www.gao.gov/archive/ 1996/he96103.pdf

U.S. Secret Service & U.S. Department of Education. (2002, May). *The final report and findings of the safe school initiative: Implications for the prevention of school attacks in the United States.* Washington, DC: Author.

Vogel, S. (1990). Gender differences in intelligence, language, visual–motor abilities, and academic achievement in students with learning disabilities: A review of the literature. *Journal of Learning Disabilities, 23*(1), 44–52.

Welsh, W. (2000). The effects of school climate on school disorder. *Annals of American Academy of Political and Social Science, 567,* 88–107.

Wenar, C., & Kerig, P. (2000). *Developmental psychopathology: From infancy through adolescence.* Boston: McGraw-Hill Higher Education.

Wolk, R. (2004). Thinking the unthinkable. *Educational Horizons, 82*(4), 268–283.

World Health Organization. (1992). *ICD-10: The classification of behavioral and mental disorders.* Geneva, Switzerland: Author.

ZTNightmares.com. (2003). *Zero tolerance nightmare stories.* Retrieved May 20, 2007, from http://ztnightmares.com/html/other_stories.htm

About the Author

Betsy Gunzelmann became interested in the differences among schools when required to change high schools after a family move. Once out in the field professionally, she observed firsthand the uniqueness of each school's climate and the children who thrived, as well as those who were not well served by their schools. She has worked for a number of years in the schools as a counselor, psychologist, and consultant. She completed her undergraduate degree in elementary education and then went on to earn two master's degrees—one in elementary education and the other in guidance and counseling. She received her doctoral degree from Boston University. Gunzelmann has been teaching at the college and graduate levels for approximately 20 years. She is chair of psychology at Southern New Hampshire University, Manchester.

www.ingramcontent.com/pod-product-compliance
Lightning Source LLC
Chambersburg PA
CBHW030654270326

41929CB00007B/356

9 781578 866908